No Crying
Allowed

Other Books by Christopher J. Knott-Craig

Lend Me a Kiss
The Weird Animal Club
Bedtime Dinosaur Stories for Kids
The Weird Animal Club at Halloween
The Weird Animal Club Goes to School

No Crying Allowed

The Journey from Farm Boy to Pediatric Cardiac Surgeon:

A Collection of Essays and Memoirs

CHRISTOPHER J. KNOTT-CRAIG, MD

This book is a work of non-fiction. Unless otherwise noted, the author and the publisher make no explicit guarantees as to the accuracy of the information contained in this book and in some cases, names of people and places have been altered to protect their privacy.

Archway Publishing books may be ordered through booksellers or by contacting:

Archway Publishing
1663 Liberty Drive
Bloomington, IN 47403
www.archwaypublishing.com
1 (888) 242-5904

Because of the dynamic nature of the Internet, any web addresses or links contained in this book may have changed since publication and may no longer be valid. The views expressed in this work are solely those of the author and do not necessarily reflect the views of the publisher, and the publisher hereby disclaims any responsibility for them.

ISBN: 978-1-4808-6352-1 (sc)
ISBN: 978-1-4808-6353-8 (e)

Library of Congress Control Number: 2018960306

Print information available on the last page.

Archway Publishing rev. date: 10/8/2018

*To my darling children—Christopher, Mary-Ann, and
Catherine—and for Connie and Danese, who have loved
and supported me through all the trials and tribulations*

"Come on, wind; make me strong"
*(Challenging the headwind to blow stronger in order
to build stamina while training for a marathon.)*

Contents

Introduction

Most young people have dreams for themselves and for their lives before society systematically tries to persuade them that they are not good enough to achieve those dreams. I am no exception. From the age of fourteen, I wanted to be a cardiac surgeon. I entered medical school already wanting to be a cardiac surgeon. When I finally started training as a cardiac surgeon, I was quickly told that I was not good enough to succeed and that I needed to do something else. But I persevered with only my dreams and my dogged determination. This book is many things, but it is essentially a telling of that journey to realize my dreams. And, along the way, I share the self-deprecating humor, experiences, and renegade thinking that have resulted in the person I am today, leading to one of the top pediatric cardiac surgery programs in the world.

1

Farm Milk Is Very Different

It was warm and thick and creamy. It landed in a bucket
that was positioned on the ground close to where the urine
landed. And I was supposed to drink this—and be excited
about it. You have got to be kidding me!

I was four years old and was on the farm with my grandparents (Ouma and Oupa, as we called them). At five thirty
in the morning my brother, Alan, and I had to help milk
the cows. We sat on stools and milked the teats, directing
the milk into stainless steel buckets that stood precariously
close to the back legs of the cow—and even closer to where
the urine landed when the cow peed. When the udders were
empty and the buckets were full, we carried the buckets to
a shallow cement pond that looked like a cement baking
pan and emptied the milk into it. A long pole centered in
the pond slowly revolved, skimming the milk of the cream
that was on top. This was used for making butter and
cheese. But before the milk was skimmed, we used a pail to
scoop out enough fresh, warm, creamy milk for breakfast.
Everyone jostled to get the first glass of warm fresh milk.
All except me, that is. For me, milk was supposed to come

from a bottle in the fridge, not from the udder of a cow I knew by name.

I could not drink it. I could not even taste it. It disgusted me. Every morning I would pretend to be full and skip breakfast. Then I would tell the African kitchen lady in the Xhosa language, "Ifuna isonka. Ifuna ibottor. Ifuna ineorbanob" ("I want bread with butter and honey"). Xhosa is the language of the largest tribe in South Africa, the one to which Nelson Mandela belonged. Mandela grew up less than two hundred miles from my grandparents' farm in Komga.

And so I faked drinking warm fresh milk. I faked it then, and I still cannot drink warm milk today. Milk should come from a bottle or a carton, not a cow! Everyone knows that, right?

2

The Sacrificial Lamb

There were sheep on my grandparents' farm, where we spent most of our holidays. In fact, there were many sheep. My oupa (grandfather) used to take my brother Alan and me to the pastures to count them as they were herded through the gate from one field to another. I was amazed at how he could accurately count a hundred or more sheep so quickly.

Of course, there were also baby sheep, or lambs, on the farm. These lambs were often taken away from their mothers and brought to a little enclosed pasture behind the house. As young children (five to seven years old), we were tasked with feeding these lambs. We had baby bottles with baby teats. We filled the bottles with the fresh warm cow milk and fed the lambs like babies, cradling them in our arms or on our laps. We named them and called them by their names, and they would run up to us when we called them. And then the lambs grew up. What we did not know was that the lambs that had been singled out for us to nurse and feed with bottles had also been singled out for the Christmas feast six weeks later. One morning, usually a couple of days before Christmas, one of the farm laborers would lead a lamb (in this case, Betsie) to a place behind the farm shed. Unknowingly, Alan and I accompanied him on this trip one day. In a flash, he unsheathed a long knife and slit Betsie's throat in a second. He hooked her up by the hind legs and suspended her from a tree limb so all the blood could drain out. I sniveled in the background, shocked and traumatized by this gruesome scene. But this was farm life for town boys. He then skinned the lamb and carved it up into manageable portions to be cooked for the Christmas feast.

I never had much of an appetite at those meals. I could still hear the bleating of the lamb that we had unknowingly raised to be the sacrificial lamb. One didn't eat one's pets, right?

Meat was supposed to come from the butcher shop, neatly wrapped in packages. Everybody knows that, right? Well, town kids know that!

3

The Railway-Track Adventure

Farm life for young boys was full of adventure. My older brother, Alan; Pop (a close friend who was a year older than Alan); and I were together each day from early morning till late at night. We practically lived together. Alan and I slept in the front room of the farmhouse, which had large windows that opened by sliding the lower half upward, not inside out like the leaf of a book like today's windows. There was no air-conditioning in those days, so we would always slide open the window about twelve inches at nighttime when we went to bed; sliding it wider than that might encourage any manner of animals to enter our room either for warmth in winter or for coolness in summer.

This crack in the window was, however, perfect for Pop to slide through at daybreak. And so on most days, he would enter through the window at five thirty in the morning and wake us up to go play. Since there was no TV or internet or mobile phones or iPads in those days, playing was real playing. It usually included a game of rugby on the grass. Since we were only three boys, we forced Frankie, Pop's younger brother, to play so that we would have two players on each side. Our days also included a trip to the club, a men's bar and lounge, which had a Ping-Pong table. Since the bar only opened around noon, we could sneak in and play Ping-Pong for a few hours each morning in the delicious surroundings of stale cigar smoke and leather upholstery and half-empty whiskey glasses. We were about ten years old but were never tempted to taste any of the leftover liquor. And since my oupa was the mayor of the town and my ouma was the headmistress of the only school, nobody at the club gave us any grief. They let us pretty much do whatever we wanted within reason.

From time to time, we invented further adventures. One of these involved Pop, Alan, and me hiking a few miles into the countryside along the railway track, looking for snakes or rabbits, scaling fences to pick the neighbor farmer's apples, and, yes, playing chicken with the trains traveling along the railway line. We would stand on the railway line facing the oncoming train and see which of the three of us was the last to jump off the track as the train raced past us, to the agitated consternation of the engine driver who was frantically gesticulating from the window. Since oupa was also the station master of the railway station in Komga, running over his grandchildren would have serious consequences. On one such occasion, I was standing with Pop and Alan facing the oncoming train, but this time I had a small Brownie camera in my hand, and I was trying to take a picture of the oncoming train. Looking at the train though the camera lens of course distorted the distance between the train and me, and had it not been for Alan jerking me by my arm, I would almost certainly have been run over. This time, the furious train driver stopped the train and chased us through the bushes before returning to the train and continuing his journey. Needless to say, it was a great adventure.

4

The Bata Toughee's Hike

I have always loved hiking, and I still do. Boy Scouts afforded me this opportunity in South Africa. One had to be eleven years old to join the Boy Scouts; younger boys could be Cubs but not Scouts. When I turned eleven, I immediately joined the Boy Scouts troop. Alan, being fifteen months older than me, was already a member, and we decided to do the unthinkable—enter for the Bata Toughee's fifty-mile hike. This hike required us to sleep outside for three nights, cook, survive the outdoors, and chronicle the hike with a logbook that included topography, vegetation, and experiences. My older brother, Alan, who was also my best friend and still is, and his peer Neil were signed up for this formidable hike, and they reluctantly agreed for me to come along as the third person. No one else was crazy enough to avail themselves of this unique opportunity.

It was summer in Oudtshoorn, the rural town where we lived (population about fourteen thousand). Oudtshoorn was located in the Karoo, a semidesert part of South Africa. The temperature easily reached 105 degrees Fahrenheit during the day. We knew this but were undeterred. And we were sorely unprepared too. Alan, Neil, and Carl all had simple backpacks, but I only had a "tog bag" to carry my gear—that is a twenty-inch-tall bag, about fourteen inches wide with a drawstring at the top that cinched the bag closed. I could then loop the drawstring over my shoulder to carry the bag. A tog bag was meant to carry a change of clothing to sports practice at school, not for hiking. *My* tog bag was stuffed with clothing, water bottles, food, provisions, and so on. It was not meant for hiking!

We set out early that morning and planned to walk sixteen miles the first day to a place called Zebra, a camping site along a shallow river sounded by blue gum trees (eucalyptus trees). There were four of us : Alan, my older brother; Carl; Neil; and me (I was the youngest). The site was owned by a benevolent farmer who had allowed the Boy Scouts to use it as a camping site in the past. The sixteen-mile hike that day in the burning sun, along the railway track, was brutal to say the least. Hiking with a heavy tog bag slung over one shoulder and a staff (head-high walking stick) in the other hand made it even more brutal. Soon my shoulder was caked in fresh blood that soaked my shirt and then dried blood. I ground my teeth, determined not to whine or complain to my older brother or his friend. At one point, Alan noticed my agony and carried my tog bag for a while to allow my shoulder to rest.

We finally reached our destination and camping spot for the night. We were all exhausted but still had two more days to go. Alan and Neil stripped down and dived into the creek to cool off. I declined, afraid they would see my shoulder, which was bleeding freely by then and aching terribly. We made a campfire; the bark of the blue gum trees was so dry that it was very easy to ignite. Then "Crane" mysteriously showed up. Crane was the Scout Master, as well as a sergeant major in the infantry. (There was an infantry training camp situated in Oudtshoorn.) He had come to check on us and had brought a live hen for us to kill, process, and cook. He explained that slaughtering and preparing a meal out of the live chicken would earn us important points toward a prize for the national competition in which we were participating. I was careful to hide my shoulder from him, wearing a T-shirt over my regular shirt to hide the blood.

First, we had to kill the hen. Alan held the chicken by the legs and stretched its neck across the stump of a tree trunk, and I held the axe that Crane had brought with him. Neil had the camera to document our culinary skills. I was very squeamish, not wanting to get any blood on me when I chopped off the head of the chicken. So I chopped the neck and jumped back at the same time. Well, this resulted in my chopping only halfway through the neck of the hen, which took off flying around in circles with Alan holding onto it by the legs. It was spewing blood everywhere, mostly onto Alan. There was a lot of cursing (from Alan) and a lot of laughing by the rest of us. Finally, the exsanguinated chicken lay dead. Then we had to "process and cook" it. We were told to first stick our fingers into the chicken's behind and retrieve the unlaid eggs (there were two) before we could cook the hen. That was so gross!

Then we made a pile of mud around the campfire using the river's soft soil. We packed the chicken in the mud until it was completely covered and then put it in the fire to cook. It seemed like it took an eternity. Of course, we had no idea how long to cook it, and our fire kept going out. And we were exhausted. And it was late at night by this time. When we finally took it out and peeled off the mud, the feathers all came off with the mud and we could eat the chicken. But without any salt or seasoning, and with the thoughts of the slaying and egg extraction fresh in our memories, we took the obligatory one bite of the chicken and that was all. Then we crawled into our sleeping bags, tired, hungry but elated.

The next morning, we cleaned up the campsite and got on our way. Crane said he was going to accompany us for a few miles just for fun. Well, we walked for about five miles along the railway track until we came to a siding where the railway forked and where the road over the Montague Pass started. This was an old, mostly untraveled road over the Outeniqua Mountain range. At this point, Crane looked at the sorry sight of the three of us—three unprepared boys doing something courageous without proper gear or food, filled only with determination and pride. My shoulder was bleeding freely again, and I had given up trying to hide it. Crane pursed his lips and told us, "No. That's enough. You are going home. You put up a great fight. Better to live to fight another day." None of us argued.

He took us home. Neil went on to finish a later fifty-mile hike and got third prize in the national competition. Alan and Carl lost interest in it and moved on intellectually. I was humiliated and burning to do the hike again under better circumstances. I would tackle it again a few years later.

5

The Bata Toughee's Hike Revisited

It was now 1969. I was sixteen, and I had never forgotten the humiliation of having to quit the hike when I was almost twelve years old. I was determined to do it again and finish. I wanted to do exactly the same route as I had done before and do it in summer just as before too. Actually, I wanted to do a longer hike than the fifty-mile requirement. The route I selected was thirty-seven miles and included a hike over a six-thousand-foot mountain pass. I would later add on a twenty-four-mile hike over a seven-thousand-foot mountain pass in the dead of winter.

So my friends Peter, Dick, Carl, and I set off. This time I was older and better prepared; I was more determined than ever before. We hiked the same route and camped at the same spot as I had four years earlier. However, after the first day of hiking and camping out, Dick and Carl decided that they had had enough and hitched a ride on a train, saying they would meet us at the beach a few days later. Peter and I continued the grueling three-day hike alone, finishing it on time. I chronicled the hike with sketches of the topography and kept samples of the vegetation. We camped out two of the nights out in the bushes. We had a wonderful time together, skinny-dipping in the river and "borrowing" apples from orchards along the way. I had walking boots and a rucksack this time around, and we had no trouble completing the itinerary. Once we met up again with Dick and Carl, we enjoyed swimming in the ocean together. But my friends had little interest in doing the second leg of the hike to complete the fifty-mile distance.

I decided to ask—or persuade—my best friend Ockie to do it with me. Ockie was a Voortrekker, the Afrikaans counterpart of the Boy Scouts. I wanted to hike over the Swartberg Mountains (6,800 feet high) in the heart of winter. It gets very cold during winter in Oudtshoorn, about thirty-six to forty degrees Fahrenheit at nighttime. We expected it to be much colder than this at altitude when we traversed the Swartberg Mountains, but this would add to the challenge. I wore a blue jersey that my mom had knitted for me because it had a long neck that could be folded over to keep my neck warm. We did not have gloves or windbreakers. We double-socked to keep our feet warm. Along the way, we met a farm laborer who had injured his hand, and we took the time to doctor him with the first aid kit we carried with us.

It was a good hike. Ockie was bigger and taller and stronger than me, but I had an unparalleled determination to succeed. We needed to camp for the night on top of the mountain, where it was bitterly cold and wet and there were eight inches of snow on the ground. So we collected a huge pile of pine needles and laid our sleeping bags on top of it to keep us off the wet, freezing ground. We slept erratically for short periods at a time. Around one o'clock in the morning, we were disturbed by a ranger who came upon us and scared the devil out of us. He told us we would die of exposure if we stayed where we were, but we were determined. He said he would take us to his lodge nearby and would not tell anyone we had slept there. But we were determined to do it the right way; this was part of the challenge that we (or rather, I) had set for ourselves, so we declined and braved the night. Of course, fires were not allowed on the mountain, making the experience even more challenging.

Very early the next morning, we got up and packed up our gear. I had brought a two-inch liquid petroleum tin burner—kind of a glorified candle. It would, however, boil just enough water in our steel mugs for a single cup of coffee for each of us. Water boils at a lower temperature at high altitudes, but even so, a warm cup of coffee would be a wonderful treat for each of us. I had also packed a small carton of milk for our coffee. Well, I made Ockie's coffee in his mug, which he was enjoying while I boiled the water in my mug. I fixed my coffee and sat down on my haunches to enjoy it when Ockie said, "Hey, Chris, you love milk, right?" With that, he filled my warm coffee mug with the cold milk, reducing my coffee to a tepid temperature. I was furious! I told him he could find his own way down the mountain because I was heading off on my own. And off I went at a blistering pace. Even though Ockie lived on a farm, this was his first real hiking experience. He was anxious and tried hard to keep up with me. But I was so mad at him for ruining my cup of coffee that I kept going fast and did not take a break, rest, or wait for him. After some three hours, we had descended sufficiently to reach a flowing rivulet. We were both exhausted and thirsty since we had used our remaining water for the coffee, but neither of us wanted to be the first to take a break. I slowed down as I approached the river, waiting for

Ockie to suggest we stop to refill our water bottles. Well, he slowed down too, waiting for me to make the suggestion. It was so silly. Both of us were being so stubborn and prideful. Finally, we looked at each other and both stopped; we simultaneously burst out laughing and raced to the river to replenish our thirst, friends again.

We finished the twenty-four-mile hike together. With the thirty-seven miles from the first leg, I had done sixty-one miles in total. I completed my logbook, writing out the logs and other information in my left-handed cursive writing. (I still have this diary.) I entered the national competition and won second prize, which was an aluminum-supported real rucksack. It was my first real rucksack, and I still have it today. In my mind, I had vindicated my earlier failure, and more importantly, I had strengthened my resolve and self-confidence in the face of adversity.

6

The Montague Pass Survival Hike

As a teenager, I was all about challenges. The harder and more arduous the challenge was, the better it was for me.

And so I decided I wanted to do a thirty-seven-mile hike over a mountain pass in the heat of summer (over 105 degrees for most of the day). I wanted to do it without resting and without food or water—well, with only a tin of condensed milk and a single water bottle of water. The challenge would require us to scrounge for water and something to eat along the way from natural sources only. The course would be Oudtshoorn to George along the Montague Pass—a sixteen-hour hike.

To accompany me, I chose Vernon, a close friend who was also a state champion athlete and rugby player. It would be just the two of us. We would each carry a backpack with toiletries, a change of clothing and some additional warm clothes, a first aid kit, a tin of condensed milk, a bottle of water, and a camera.

We left around noon in the heat of the day and followed the railway line from Oudtshoorn to the Zebra railway siding outpost. All was well, and we both were holding up well. We filled our water bottles at Zebra from the brook and hiked to the foot of the Outeniqua Mountain range. We would skirt Cradock Peak, which stood about 6,500 feet. We started the ascent along the Montague Pass around eight o'clock that evening along a mostly abandoned dust road. The course became colder, much colder, and very dark. We did not have torches (flashlights), and even following the course of the road was difficult. We really could not see anything in front of us. We reached the highest point of the pass around midnight; passed the overhead railway bridge, which was supposed to be haunted; and then started the descent toward George, our destination. Around one thirty in the morning, Vernon said he was exhausted, thirsty, and miserable. By then, we had long been out of water or anything to eat. To help him, I took his backpack, added it on top of mine, and carried both for the rest of the way. About an hour later, Vernon lay down on his back in the road and refused to move or continue the journey; he was exhausted and wasn't moving. He said he would wait till morning and hitch a ride with a farmer, who was sure to be traveling the road.

Well, this was thirty years before cell phones or any other means of communicating. And I could not leave him alone on the mountain, especially in the state he was in. But I did not want to give up on the challenge either! I helped Vernon up, slung his arm around my neck and shoulders, and supported him down the mountain. With frequent resting and slow progress, it took us another four hours to descend and stagger into George. We stopped at the local hospital on the outskirts of George, where the doctors revitalized Vernon. I was able to make a phone call to my dad there, and I asked him if he could send someone to fetch us. We had planned to take the train back, but neither of us was in any shape to do that at this point.

Well, we had completed the challenge and the hike, and both of us were no worse for the wear. Although Vernon and I have remained friends for fifty years, we have never revisited this hike or discussed it again. Nor has he ever again agreed to join me on any further challenges—not that I blame him. But for me, failure was never an option.

7

Jewelry for My Mother

I have always loved jewelry. If I am at the mall for an hour or two or in an airport waiting for a flight, I usually find myself in a bookstore or browsing in a jewelry store. I especially love diamonds, Mikimoto pearls, aquamarine stones, and blue sapphire stones. I have bought all these and designed the settings of many of the pieces of jewelry I have bought. Yes, I love beautiful jewelry.

Even as an eight-year-old child, I loved jewelry. I used to save up my pocket money each week, seldom buying sweets like my brothers and friends. We received our pocket money from my dad on a Friday. I preferred to save up this pocket money to buy jewelry, most often for my mother. The first two pieces of jewelry I bought were both for her.

I received about three cents of pocket money a week. It seems like nothing today, but we could buy a lot of candy with this back then and even an occasional drink. I saved about half of my pocket money each month and kept it in a cloth handkerchief tied in a knot at a corner. This was long before cloth handkerchiefs were replaced with disposable tissues.

At the beginning of each month, I would walk the two

miles across town to Skelly's all-purpose store. In addition to cheap toys, goods, appliances, and tinned foods, they also had a display cabinet with inexpensive jewelry locked inside. In that cabinet was a blue necklace that I had seen on an earlier trip. It had an octagonal green semiprecious stone surrounded by similar oblong stones on each side strung on a thin chain. The large octagonal stone was the largest in this string and was at the bottom of the string, and on either side the stones got smaller and smaller until only the string with the clasp remained. I loved it and wanted to buy it for my mom. An identical necklace with blue stones was next to it; I loved them both, but I liked the green one the best.

Each month I would walk to the store, which took almost an hour in the heat of the day, and I would ask to look at the necklace and touch it. The owner of the store was a good friend of my mother's, so she would get out the necklace for me to admire. Then she would unknot my handkerchief and count out my pennies. "Not enough yet," she would say over and over again. And then I would return the next month, and she would count out my money again. Finally, I had enough. I proudly paid for the first piece of jewelry I ever bought. I was eight years old, and the necklace cost one shilling and eleven pence (nineteen cents). I remember clearly the evening when I gave it to my mom. She cried with delight and pride. She loved it and wore it regularly when she went out.

She kept the necklace even after she retired to an old-age home and later a frail-care facility. And fifty-five years later, she gave the same necklace to my darling daughter, Cate, in its original box and with the same love and enthusiasm with which she had received it over a half century earlier. Cate loves it too. At some point, I also bought my mother the identical blue necklace, which she has subsequently given to Cate as well.

8

The First Ring I Bought

I bought my first two pieces of jewelry when I was eight years old for my mother, but I bought my first piece of jewelry for a girlfriend when I was ten. I was in standard three (fifth grade), and the jewelry I bought was a clear crystal in a solitaire setting. It was beautiful and the first ring I had ever bought. I bought it for my girlfriend, Rosanne. Actually, she wasn't really my "girlfriend"—just kinda sorta. In reality, I loved the ring and just needed to give it to a girl. Rosanne was the sister of my friend Raymond. He and I were both ten years old and played together all the time. His younger sister was nine.

The ring looked like a beautiful diamond even though it was a clear crystal stone. It was placed in a solitaire setting (still my favorite setting) and mounted on a fake yellow gold band. It cost twenty-five cents. But I loved it and wanted to buy it for someone. I always was a romantic and still am. And Rosanne was the unsuspecting recipient.

I brought it home and took it with me when I went to play with Raymond. I waited for my moment, and when Raymond went out of the room to do something, I excitedly gave the ring in its box to Rosanne. She opened it and exclaimed excitedly. She said, "Gee, thanks," and ran off to show everyone. Well, everyone included her older brother, who asked to look at it carefully. He then took it and deliberately flushed it down the toilet to his sister's chagrin and to my fury. Needless to say, a fistfight broke out between Raymond and me, which I won. I was so mad at him! But the ring was gone.

Raymond and I did not remain friends much longer, and Rosanne and I were not special friends anymore either. But thus started a long habit of buying beautiful jewelry pieces and giving them to special friends. It's the same today, half a century later.

9

Sunday Lunch in the Bushveld

I don't eat liver—ever. I don't like liver. I don't like the smell of cooked liver. And I don't eat cooked liver. I never have, not even as a fourteen-year-old boy in an area of northern South Africa called the bushveld, a part of Northern Transvaal.

I was visiting a farm near Messina in the rural part of northern South Africa. My older brother, Alan, and I were having a vacation with my aunt's family. In the bushveld, hunting and farming were the major industries. This was around 1968. The rule of law was the rifle. Rifles were used for hunting and putting food on the table, for leisure, and to resolve any dispute; the police were rarely, if ever, seen in this part of the world.

There was the rifle and the "sambok." The sambok was a braided cowhide whip about six feet long and an inch wide that tapered down to a thin end. It was used in lieu of the rifle on pets, house servants, laborers—and unruly children. The sambok was to be sorely feared. It brought to life the meaning to the biblical phrase "Spare the rod and spoil the child." There were very few "spoiled" children on the farm. Children obeyed their parents the first time they were asked to do a chore. There was no back-chatting, no sulking, and no time-outs—just the sambok or the threat of it. Also on the farm was Frikkie. Frikkie was a huge twenty-two-year-old (or thereabouts—no one knew for sure) man with Down syndrome. Frikkie weighed over three hundred pounds, walked around barefoot and in only shorts, and ate outside with the pets. And he was controlled with the sambok, as we witnessed several times during our six-week stay on the farm. Alan and I were very well mannered during our visit; we never argued, and we were asked only once to do a chore. We had seen the sambok at work, and we wanted no part of it.

Well, one Sunday, we all sat down together to have lunch as a "family." Sunday lunch was a formal institution to be revered by all. It started with solemn prayers followed by a big meal, and everyone had to clean his or her plate by eating everything on it. After all, it was a privilege to have food on the table. And by God, you showed your appreciation by eating it all. Meat was the staple of the farm diet, and usually it was very tasty, even delicious, including lamb or beef loin chops basted in mayonnaise and salt and pepper. However, roast potatoes, cooked pumpkin, squash, and all those good vegetables that are grown on the farm are universally avoided by teenager boys, like Alan and me.

Well, we had had an energetic morning filled with lots of activity, and by the time Sunday lunch came, we were starving. We had to go change into Sunday clothes, wash our faces and hands, and come to the dining room table, where we sat down waiting for prayers and a feast. All the vegetables were already set out on the table—sweet potatoes, which I still cannot stomach; pumpkin, which to this day I do not eat; and roast potatoes, which I love—and then there was the major part of the meal being carried in on a huge platter: the meat dish. Before the cook entered the room with the platter, I could already smell that malodorous smell of grilled liver diced into one-inch-square pieces. I was ready to throw up. Alan, on the other hand, was involved in an animated conversation with our uncle Johan. Alan is not only color blind but also has a much less refined sense of smell. He was so involved in his discussion that he failed to smell that unmistakable liver odor, and it would be fair to say that we both abhorred liver equally. Well, Alan was telling everyone at the table that he was starving, and so the hostess, my great-aunt—the one who usually brandished the sambok and ruled the house—dished a pile of liver into his plate. I, on the other hand, having summed up the situation in a split second, feigned a severe tummy ache and asked if I could have only some potatoes to help settle it. Well, when Alan eagerly put the first bite of grilled liver in his mouth and realized it was liver and not meat, he turned green. Then he gave me the most threatening look imaginable. His face said, *I'm going to kill you for not warning me.* I was trying my hardest to suppress my laughter. With tears rolling down my cheeks, I munched on my roast potatoes as I watched Alan painfully eat every piece of that disgusting liver, his eyes never leaving my face but reflecting nausea, anger, and retribution to come.

But the best was yet to come. When he finally finished his plate of liver with the determination and courage and perseverance that only an insane fear of the sambok could engender, our great-aunt asked him if he would like some more. He replied, "No, thank you, ma'am. It was delicious." She answered, "Oh, my boy, you don't have to be shy," and she filled his plate up a second time with more "delicious" liver. At this point I could not contain my laughter any longer and fled the room. I figured that whatever beating my older brother was going to give me when he caught up with me was worth it!

10

Cricket

We played cricket at school—in junior school, in high school, after school, and during recess. Cricket was to us what soccer is to the rest of the world, and we all wanted to play. It was a game predominantly played by the English-speaking school kids, although since we made up only 25 percent of the school population, our team included mostly Afrikaans-speaking boys. We followed the Springboks, our national cricket team, and knew all the players by name. This was the era of great South African teams, with players the like of Procter, the Pollock brothers, Lindsay, and Goddard, among others.

Since my dad was the editor of several country newspapers and the sports correspondent for all the national Sunday newspapers, we were in the privileged position of often knowing the national cricket stars on a personal level. As an example, the famous cricketer Mike Procter stayed at our home over weekends while he was doing his compulsory military training in Oudtshoorn. He used to bowl to us in the backyard on our cement pitch. Peter and Graeme Pollock fetched Alan and me in Port Elizabeth to be their guests in the VIP box during the game between Natal and Eastern Province in 1968.

Yes, we were very motivated to play cricket for our school. Alan and I played on the same team for several years. Alan was a fast bowler, and at other times he was the wicket keeper. I was the opening batsman and a left-hand off-spin bowler. We had practice on Tuesdays and Thursdays after school from four to six o'clock. Although we officially had a coach, Alan and I usually ran the practices, rotating bowlers and batsmen and so on. We also collected all the gear before and after practice and carried it across the field to the storage room, quite a distance away.

Saturday was game day. Games usually started at nine in the morning and ended at six in the evening. Before each game, all the clobber had to be brought out, cleaned, and laid out. The pitch had to be mowed with a hand-pushed lawn mower and rolled twenty times on each strip; there were six strips on the pitch. We used a heavy steel roller that had to be pulled the twenty-four paces of the pitch. It normally took two people to pull it, but since most days only Alan and I were preparing the pitch, one of us pulled the roller and the other mowed the pitch. We started soon after six in the morning and finished preparing the pitch and painting it just in time for the match to start. Then the match would be played in one-hundred-degree heat for eight hours, including the hour-long break for lunch. Alan and I both played well and made the provincial (regional or state) side for multiple years. But the toll of the coaching, preparing the field, cleaning up afterward, and still performing well during the matches took a toll on both of us. After five years at high school, neither of us ever played cricket again, except for a casual pickup game at university.

If it is possible to be burnt out playing the game you love at high school, then we were both burnt out by the time we graduated. But I still have my clobber from back then.

11

Boot Camp in the South African Infantry

Back then, all men in South Africa had to do a compulsory two-year stint in the armed forces. For most college graduates, this meant the army.

My two-year period started in January 1979 after I graduated from medical school and completed my one-year internship. All of us physicians and dentists and other degreed graduates were placed in the same boot camp for three months before we were deployed in the medical corps. It was brutal. The noncommissioned officers (NCOs) in charge of us were invariably unschooled and saw this as an opportunity to show "those college assholes" who ruled the roost. At one point, seven physicians were simultaneously being treated in the military intensive care unit with heat stroke, kidney failure, and so on. Because we had degrees, we would all be officers when we finished boot camp. But until then, we were at the mercy of the NCOs who ran the boot camp. The leader was a sadistic staff sergeant named Kemp. He epitomized brutality and seemed to revel in seeing "these fancy, clever jerks" get injured or worse. He was rumored to have been demoted for employing these same antics on his fellow paratroopers, who finally tossed him out of the helicopter across enemy lines—hence his bitterness and mission to get even and teach us a lesson or two.

On several occasions, he would force all two hundred of us in the boot camp to hold our rifles at arm's length in front of us in the hundred-degree heat until at least five people fainted. Then we would have to run up a long, sandy hill and back repeatedly. When everyone was totally wasted, he would make the last twenty do it over and make the rest of us watch as our friends collapsed or lost consciousness without being allowed to help them. He was careful to have a couple of ambulances nearby to resuscitate them from the brink of death, although, as I stated before, there were at one point seven people in the intensive care unit. And there was no recourse. There were no cell phones or internet, mail was not allowed, and we had no way to alert our families as to what was transpiring. It was a nightmare. We lived on peanut-butter-and-honey sandwiches. We tried to bribe the corporals to alert our parents, but we were unsuccessful since they were all terrified of Staff Sergeant Kemp too.

Boot camp ended with a three-day, two-night march in the hills out somewhere far away from any civilization or prying eyes. This was Kemp's last opportunity to teach us a lesson before we graduated; after graduation from boot camp, he would have to salute and take orders from us. Each day, we needed to march a course navigated with compasses during the day and the stars at night. This was the middle of summer; the temperatures regularly exceeded one hundred degrees Fahrenheit during the day. Our rations for each twenty-four-hour period were restricted to a third of a tin of canned beetroot each and a single water bottle filled with a liter of water. That's it. I was the leader of my platoon of some fourteen people. I was somewhat used to survival hikes and rationing, so I would save some of my water for the weakest member of my platoon. Each day, the march was about sixteen miles of hills with very little shade. When we got back to camp at night, we would have our fill of water, and the cooks would have prepared a huge meal for us to eat. There would also be a huge hole dug in the ground between the food and us. And just as we would get ready to line up to get food, Kemp would "accidentally" knock over the food containers into the hole and laugh as they buried the food. That way, they could show anyone who asked that they had prepared food for the troops and only wasted what was not eaten.

On the second day of the march, my platoon came upon a puddle of water about six feet wide and three inches deep that had developed from a rain shower the previous night. A cow stood at the edge of the puddle, urinating. The cow had finished drinking, and its urine trickled back into the puddle. My platoon was so thirsty that they ran to the puddle, knelt beside it, and drank the muddy water, urine and all. That's how desperate we were. On the third day, I said to my platoon, "We have to outsmart those pigs! We are smarter. We have college degrees!" We marched for the third day having each only eaten two thirds of one tin of canned beetroot over the previous two days. In the distance, I saw a farmhouse. I told my platoon to stay put and watch me. I took one other member with me, a strong man who looked to be in the best shape. We took off our packs, tied four water bottles around our necks, and jogged the mile or so to the farmhouse.

We persuaded the kind farm lady to fill our water bottles. She also gave us some cheese, boiled eggs, and bread, and we jogged back to the platoon with our prize meal. Everyone cheered and laughed, even though we knew that if Kemp found out we would be in serious trouble, whatever that meant in this context. It revitalized our platoon and our morale.

The final morning, we lined up at breakfast after the three-day-long "we will break them" march. Staff Sergeant Kemp now had a problem: he had all this food that had not been eaten and was bound to be questioned about it. So he had the cooks prepare a massive breakfast for us of bacon, eggs, oatmeal porridge, bread, peanut butter, honey, and more.

We knew we were returning to camp straight after breakfast and would at least be fed there. So I and the other ten platoon leaders communicated with one another and decided on the following plan. It was childish but hugely satisfying to all of us. When Kemp blew the whistle for everyone to join in the breakfast feast, everyone shouted at the top of their lungs, "Fuck you! You can't break us! And next week you will salute us!" And all gave him the finger.

Well, all the food was poured into holes in the ground, and we were ordered to cover up the holes with dirt. We didn't care, although it was very hard to resist grabbing a piece of bacon. But we did not want to give Kemp the satisfaction of seeing us eat. That's how we finished the hardest three months of my life.

12

Confronting the Enemy

It was well over one hundred degrees during most of the day in the Caprivi Strip, the northernmost strip of land separating the armed forces of South Africa and South West Africa (now named Namibia) from the enemy—the South West African People's Organisation (SWAPO) and the communist-supported regime of Angola. A fierce struggle was going on between these two forces, and the United States was covertly supporting the South African forces, who were aligned with the rebel leader, Sawimbi. The Union of Soviet Socialist Republics (USSR) was supporting the Angolan regime, who had its eyes on the lucrative diamond mines of Namibia. The South African forces were stationed south of the border along the Caprivi Strip, surrounded by the Okavango swamps and separated from Angola by the Cubango River. This river varied in width from one hundred yards wide in places to four hundred yards in others. And along the Caprivi Strip, there was only one road running its length, between Rundu and Katima Mulilo.

I was driving the army jeep along this "golden highway" with the army chaplain, who was also a two-star lieutenant.

We had our FN rifles with us, and our pistols were in their holsters on our sides. We were sweating profusely in the summer heat, so we decided to stop and have a swim in the Cubango River to cool off since there was not a person in sight and we were drenched on this deserted dust road. We stopped the jeep on the bank of the river and stripped down naked. We waded into the deliciously cool river, not caring about possible hippos or crocodiles. The water was so refreshing. Unselfconsciously we enjoyed the river together—two officers of the South African army on the front lines during a vicious war.

Then we froze. Directly in front of us on the opposite bank of the river, no more than seventy yards from us, were seven members of the opposing forces with their AK-47 rifles aimed directly at us. They had materialized out of nowhere. We were looking into the face of certain death. The opposing forces were given monetary incentives for "kills," and officer kills were especially well rewarded. It was over for us. We stared at them, waiting for the hail of bullets to hit us.

"If you should survive, tell my wife I love her," I whispered to the chaplain. "I'll do the same for you."

"What do we do now?" he asked.

Well, we turned around and slowly walked back to our jeep, some thirty yards away, bracing for the bullets that were sure to pierce our backs. But no shots were fired. We got to the jeep, donned our military uniforms, and strapped our pistols to our sides, never looking at the enemy. We got into the jeep and quickly glanced across the river. The seven guerilla soldiers were still standing there with their rifles aimed at us, but for some unfathomable reason, no one fired at us. We drove for a couple of miles and then stopped, shaking uncontrollably. We knew that we should have been dead.

We knew that we had been saved by divine intervention. Maybe those soldiers looked at us and thought how nice it would be to take a dip in the river themselves. Who knows. It's a mystery to this day.

13

The Abdominal IV Catheter

It was 1978. I was doing my two-year compulsory army service that all males in South Africa had to do. I was a full lieutenant in the medical corps and was deployed at an army base in the Caprivi Strip on northern Namibia. I was one of two medical doctors or dentists who were deployed at any one time at this camp, the 31st Battalion. Our hospital was a single gazebo room with very little of anything useful.

Stationed in this camp were the South African soldiers and the Vasquela Bushmen tribe and their families. The Bushmen were a pigmy race, olive-skinned and small with an incredible tracking ability. The army relied on them to track the enemy in this semidesert area. The Bushmen loved their families, especially their children. One never saw or heard of any bushman hurting or abusing his children— this was unthinkable! Among the traditions of the Bushmen tribe was the belief that if a death occurred in the home, the home had to be burned to the ground and a new home built. We are talking about a tepee-type home, made from sticks and skins, not bricks and mortar.

So, if an infant or child became ill, first the family would call the *sangoma*, or witch doctor, who would often make some cuts on the infant's chest, dance, and throw bones in order to ward off the evil spirits who had caused the illness. But, very often, the infant had developed gastroenteritis and was in extremis, so after the witch doctor had exhausted all his medicine, the father would pick up the infant and run to the hospital so that the baby would die in the hospital and not in his home, thereby preventing the need to burn down his home and build a new one.

I witnessed this several times during the three months I was stationed there. It was sad and very frustrating not being able to treat these infants. Although we had IV fluids to resuscitate soldiers injured in battle, we had none that were suitable for a baby. The smallest IV was sixteen-gauge, which is good for an adult but way too big for a baby, especially a baby who was dehydrated to the point of death.

One afternoon, a father brought in his six-month-old baby who was severely dehydrated and in extremis. *Gastro,* I thought, just like all the others I had seen and buried. The father wailed and cried and pleaded that the *makuo* (white man) save his baby. Then he ran away sobbing. In desperation, I took the sixteen-gauge IV, stuck it in the baby's abdomen, and started running in IV fluids. Amazingly, I had avoided the intestines, and the baby started absorbing the fluid in his abdomen, which proved to be life-saving. When the father returned the next day to fetch his supposedly dead baby, he found the infant sitting up and playing on the floor. The father cried out in disbelief and was overcome by gratitude. He took his baby home and returned with his bow and arrows as a thank you gift. This represented his entire livelihood to provide for his family, but nothing would convince him that it was totally unnecessary.

When I returned to South Africa and started working in the emergency room at Groote Schuur Hospital, I told the story to the ER physicians, who were amazed and astounded at the innovation. Needless to say, using the peritoneal cavity soon became an acceptable and standard way of resuscitating infants in difficult situations.

14

My First Cardiac Operation— on a Pigeon

I remember my father coming home from work one day unusually excited. This was in September 1967, when I was fourteen years old and in the ninth grade. A surgeon who had grown up in the area had visited his office and predicted that he would soon transplant the heart of a dead person into the chest of a desperately ill patient. He was animated, enthusiastic, and dead serious about this, my father said.

He showed me a picture of this surgeon, and I listened, mesmerized by this account from my father. My father had a bad stammer that was made worse by excitement, and that day he was verbally crippled as he told me about Professor Christiaan Barnard. I think I decided that same day to be a heart surgeon. I felt a rush of adrenaline just thinking about it. Whether I would have the ability to be a cardiac surgeon was not an issue; I could feel it in my bones, and I wanted it so badly. Soon thereafter, my neighborhood friend Leslie Drake came over to play, and we talked about my fascination with Professor Barnard and cardiac surgery.

A few days later, Leslie related that one of his dad's prize racing pigeons was ill. He had a grain stuck in his crop (throat) causing obstruction and would die unless it was fixed. I vaguely recall that the only people who knew that the pigeon was sick were the two of us. I am sure that Leslie's dad, a veteran pigeon collector and racer, did not share our concern for the health of his racing pigeon. In fact, when he left that same day, the unfortunate pigeon was perfectly fine.

Well, I knew this was serious. A life was at stake, and I had to act decisively. So Leslie and I walked the two miles to a pharmacy and bought some chloroform for anesthetic, some catgut suture material, swabs, and a scalpel. In those days, no one raised an eyebrow or questioned our intentions. When we returned to my home, we cleaned a spare kitchen table in the back room, which was used by the house servants as sleeping quarters. Then we prepared for surgery. We tore some of my mother's bedsheets into strips for surgical clothing—this was serious business and we needed to do it right!

The unsuspecting pigeon was placed on the operating table, and I held a cotton ball soaked in chloroform against his beak until all resistance ceased. With a mask on, but not gloves, I opened the bird's throat and explored my patient. Leslie was my inquisitive, though somewhat argumentative, assistant. I decided that the problem was not the crop but the heart, and so I proceeded to open the pigeon's chest and examine the heart, which I removed from the chest and later placed in a bottle. Then we checked his stomach, which we also removed and placed in a bottle too. We proceeded to suture the pigeon closed, which we did a little more hurriedly out of concern for our patient. We were not at all influenced by the garden man who had looked through the window, seen what we were up to, and yelled that he was going to phone our mothers and that we would get a *moerse pakslae* (big thrashing) when they got home.

Needless to say, the unfortunate pigeon did not recover from the procedure and was therefore buried out in the veld (countryside) where no one could find him. I was understandably very tired from the difficult surgery, so I declined the invitation to accompany Leslie to his house to tell his dad that his prize pigeon had died despite our heroic efforts. When I saw Leslie again the following day, he seemed a little stiff and sore and had a number of welts on his behind. He was also much less enthusiastic about repeating our endeavors on any other pigeons. In fact, all the other sick pigeons had amazingly recovered overnight.

But my enthusiasm was undaunted. Our biology teacher, Mr. Krab Karstens, was very appreciative of the bottle containing the stomach and the heart of the dead pigeon, which we presented to him for teaching purposes, even though he hurriedly insisted that I take it back home with me the same day in the interests of science and history! The most excited audience was my grandfather, who examined the bottle most carefully when he later visited us and assured me that I had a certain gift, for sure. He never did tell me what exactly this gift was, but it was at this point that he stopped encouraging me to become an astronaut and started telling me about his ailments, especially the surgical ones.

Some ten years later, in 1977, I graduated with a degree in medicine and started my internship with the same Professor Barnard on the cardiac surgery service of Groote Schuur Hospital in Cape Town, where he had done the first heart transplant nine years earlier. And in 1986, I qualified as a cardiothoracic surgeon myself (summa cum laude). Several years later I was considered for the chair of cardiac surgery in Cape Town after Professor Barnard had retired. Throughout my career, Christiaan Barnard was very good to me; I contributed to his biography, *Chris Barnard by Those Who Knew Him*, and we remained friends until his death in 2001. His son Andre and I were good friends too, and we both trained together to be physicians.

My first cardiac operation, inspired by the thought of transplanting a human heart from one person to another, still remains a vivid memory in my bid to become a fully fledged cardiac surgeon. And in 1994, I performed my first successful heart transplant in Oklahoma City.

15

The Importance of Perseverance

Since I was in ninth grade in high school at fourteen years old, I have wanted to be a heart surgeon. I had followed Professor Chris Barnard's career and first heart transplant in December 1967, and I wanted to be like him and to work for him. And I wanted him to know who I was.

Well, I finished high school in 1971 and medical school in 1977. Then I volunteered to be Professor Barnard's intern for two months in 1978. At that time, he had the reputation of a ferocious, scathingly critical man who was to be feared and avoided at all costs; thus, the intern slots were usually vacant. I was in heaven! I became Professor Christiaan Barnard's intern and was on my way to a career in cardiac surgery.

Following my intern year, I started my cardiac surgery residency in 1980 at Tygerberg Hospital, the sister hospital to Groote Schuur Hospital, where Professor Barnard worked. I thought I would get more practical experience there; at Groote Schuur, the residents spent most of their training watching and not doing surgery, and as a result, many were not very good surgeons. I wanted to be a good surgeon.

So I started my training under Professor Pieter Barnard at Tygerberg Hospital (no relation to Professor Christiaan Barnard). The senior faculty there included Dr. Dewet Lubbe and, later, Dr. Johan Rossouw, who was still training at the time. Many of the difficult surgeries were done by Dr. Jean-Marie Van Caster, a Belgian cardiac surgeon who was a great help and mentor to the young trainees. I started in January 1980. In June of that year, Professor Barnard called me into his office. "Chris," he said in Afrikaans (the Dutch derivative language spoken at the institution), "Dr. Rossouw and some of the other faculty say that you will never make it as a cardiac surgeon. You are left-handed, and you cannot tie surgical knots with your right hand; you are awkward operating, and you are very slow. Now, I think you are a very bright young doctor with an exceptional knowledge of cardiology. Why don't you train as a cardiologist instead? I think that's the best thing for you." I was devastated. At that time, there were no left-handed instruments; I had to learn to use the instruments backward. Nevertheless, this was the reality. I wanted to fix hearts, not diagnose what was wrong with them. I wanted to be a cardiac surgeon, like Chris Barnard. I wanted this very badly. "Sir, can you please just give me three more months to improve, please, sir?" I pleaded. After pondering, he reluctantly acquiesced.

With a sick feeling in the pit of my stomach, I went home. I was too embarrassed to tell my wife. I took home the leftover suture material from the operating room and some needle holders and forceps that the operating room matron had kindly snuck to me. At that time, the residents were working one-hundred-hour weeks in the hospital. Despite this, when I got home, I practiced tying knots over and over and over, using the bareback struts of the dining room chairs around which to tie, for hours each day, irrespective of how tired I was. I got better, and I learned to operate better. I worked harder than all my fellow residents just to try to get an edge. In South Africa, there was the pyramid system, meaning that only a third or so of those who started their residency training were allowed to finish.

I graduated in 1986, ahead of my fellow residents, and with summa cum laude, and the highest recorded score in the history of the university. I was awarded the medal for the best surgical graduate of any surgical specialty for that year. My career as a cardiac surgeon was launched but only because my professor had allowed me a second chance and an extra three months to improve—and because I could not accept failure.

Several years later, the faculty member who had told my professor that I was not cut out to be a surgeon, almost ending my career before it had started, asked me for a recommendation letter for him when he was applying for a new position., Even though the irony of this request was not lost on me, I fulfilled it. I remembered the importance of being afforded a second chance.

16

Cardiac Trauma during a Barbecue

On a Friday night in 1987, I was having a *braai* (barbecue) with my brother-in-law Jan and his family at my home in Pinelands, Cape Town. I was not on call that night, for a change, so we were enjoying some red wine, grilling lamb chops, and telling stories and laughing when my phone rang. It was the emergency room (casualty department) physician. He said he could not reach my associate, Wynand, who was on call. They had brought in an eighteen-year-old man with a stab wound to the heart; he was still alive but barely. He would not survive much longer, maybe just minutes. Could I help him? I was barefoot (my usual), in rugby shorts and a cutout T-shirt. I had already had two glasses of wine, and my lamb chops were on the grill.

"Take him into the operating room, and do not intubate him," I told him. "I'll be there in two minutes." The hospital was just down the road from my house, and there was no traffic at this time. "Jan, watch my chops and don't let my bloody meat burn," I said as I raced out the door. I ran into the operating room in the same clothes, not having time to change into scrubs or put on shoes. The patient had a barely palpable pulse, but his pupils were still reactive, suggesting that he was still alive. But there was no anesthetist—he had not yet shown up. A scrub nurse was there with a thoracotomy tray and instruments, but no other doctor was in the room! A medical student excited to be witnessing this story unfold stood next to me.

"Can you intubate this patient?" I asked him.

"I think so, sir," he said.

"Well, do it then. It's the hole in front" (as opposed to the esophagus, which is behind when the mouth is opened. We had no drugs to give the patient, and by then he was lifeless. While the medical student intubated and bagged the patient, I opened the chest on the left side, opened the pericardium (sac around the heart) and closed the hole in the right ventricle. My only assistant was the scrub nurse, who had never seen a heart before. Just then the anesthetist came in and said he would take over the anesthetic.

"Can you suture?" I asked the shell-shocked medical student.

"I think so, sir. I did some suturing in the casualty department over weekends."

"Well, scrub your hands and come close the g--d---- chest. My lamb chops are burning," I told him. Then I raced back to my car and sped home, twenty minutes after I had left the house.

The patient recovered and survived just fine, and my meat was not ruined at all. We had more wine and cursed my colleague for not answering his phone when he was on call. And when I thought of it later, I laughed at the look of shock on the scrub nurse's face when she saw me enter the operating room in shorts and without a mask or shoes on.

17

Simultaneous Cardiac Surgery on Two Brothers

Bad things happen on Friday nights. People get paid, and they go out drinking and get into fights, where someone ends up dying or badly injured due to trauma. In Cape Town in the 1980s, this usually meant a stab wound to the heart or lungs. When I analyzed the incidence of cardiac trauma at Tygerberg Hospital in Cape Town, the peak of the cardiac trauma was between 9:00 p.m. and 4:00 a.m. on a or Friday or Saturday night.

This Friday night in 1986 was no different. I got called around nine-thirty with a probable stab wound to the heart and cardiac tamponade. As usual, I asked if the patient had a pulse and whether he was intubated. If he was intubated, I would drive slowly to the hospital knowing he would be dead by the time I arrived. If, on the other hand, he was not intubated, I raced to the hospital without stopping for any red lights because I knew I had a chance to save him with emergency surgery. What I had learned was that a stab wound to the heart affected the cardiac output by causing cardiac tamponade (pressure of the blood in the sac around the heart squeezing the heart to the point that it could not eject enough blood to keep the patient alive). Although nothing was usually intrinsically wrong with the lungs in most cases, part of the protocol for resuscitation included intubation and placing the patient on a ventilator. The extra pressure from the lungs on the heart after intubation usually resulted in acute further decompensation and immediate death within minutes.

This patient was not intubated. Great. I directed the staff to take him directly into the operating room—no X-rays or blood work, I said—as I raced to the hospital. When I arrived in the operating room, the patient barely had a pulse or a recordable blood pressure. He was not moving, just panting away. I rapidly donned the surgical clothes, poured iodine over his left chest, and picked up the scalpel while the anesthetist intubated him. I cut the left front of his chest just below his nipple and opened his chest between the ribs. There was very little bleeding because he had a very low blood pressure. The scrub nurse was my only assistant, doubling as a surgical assistant and theater sister (scrub tech). I opened the pericardium, relieved the cardiac tamponade, and sutured the stab wound in the right ventricle. As his blood pressure recovered, I slowed the IV fluids and gave some Lasix to prevent heart failure. It took no more than ten minutes.

Just as I sutured his heart and it looked like he may make it, I got called directly into the operating room; another patient, also a late teenager, had just been brought into the emergency room with a stab wound to the heart. He was in extremis and needed a surgeon immediately. "Bring him into my operating room," I said. They wheeled him into the operating room, but he lost his pulse and arrested right away. Shit! "Intubate him," I said to the anesthesiologist, and then I turned to the scrub nurse and said, "Give me fresh gloves and betadine." A medical student onlooker in the operating room bagged the first patient while the anesthetist intubated the second patient on his emergency room trolley. I opened his chest with the same instruments as I had used for the first patient. I opened his pericardium and massaged his heart till it kicked in again. Then I sutured the stab wound in the right ventricle. While they placed an IV in his arm to give him some fluids, I turned around and started closing the chest of the first patient. Once I finished, I had him wheeled out of the operating room to the ICU. Then, we transferred the second patient onto the operating table and proceeded to close his chest and then transfer him to the ICU.

Both patients survived without significant complications or infections. It turned out that they were brothers. They were walking home together when a man approached them for money. They refused, and the man then stabbed them both in the chest. The first victim collapsed as an ambulance passed by. His brother told them to take his brother, who was barely conscious, to the emergency room. Some twenty minutes later, the ambulance returned to find the second brother in shock and unconscious, and they raced him to hospital. So the two brothers had been stabbed by the same person, taken separately to the same hospital by the same ambulance team, and operated on by the same surgeon in the same operating room at the same time. And they recovered side by side in ICU, both to make a full recovery.

Needless to say, the story made the front page of the newspaper.

18

Coming of Age in the Operating Room

It was 1985, and I was getting ready to do my first repair of Tetralogy of Fallot on a fifteen-month-old little boy. It was during the last two years of my residency training in cardiothoracic surgery. I had done many valve surgeries and a few coronary bypass operations, but I had not done any congenital heart surgeries other than simple atrial septal defects. These more complex operations were mostly done by the senior surgeon; I had assisted him with several of them but had never done one myself. At that time, repair of Tetralogy of Fallot was about the most complex congenital heart operation we were doing at Tygerberg Hospital. But I was ready! I had prepared well, and the senior surgeon promised to take me through this daunting operation.

As usual, I waited until the surgeon arrived at the hospital before getting the patient prepped and draped for the operation. When he arrived in the operating room, he asked if I would open the chest for him since he had a bit of a cold. "Sure," I said excitedly. When I had the chest open and the pericardial cradle completed, he asked if I could put the baby on bypass (connect cannulas to the heart and connect these to the bypass machine). "Yes, sir," I said with a little trepi-dation. I had not yet placed a baby on bypass without close supervision, but I did not want to show my anxiety; after all, he was standing right there in the operating room next to me and was getting ready to scrub and help me.

I was operating with an intern as my only assistant, and he was just learning how to hold the instruments and how to assist in surgery. When I finished successfully connecting the baby to the bypass machine, at the point of no return, I proudly turned to the senior surgeon and said, "Okay, mae-stro, we are ready for you!"

"I am not going to scrub on this case anymore. I don't feel well. I have a cold. You'll have to do it by yourself," he said. At that moment, I realized that I had been set up to fail. It felt like I had been punched in the stomach. Here I was with a baby who was going to die unless I could rebuild his heart by myself, and I had to do it without any competent assistant and without having ever done it or anything similar ever before.

I calmed my racing heart, said a silent prayer, placed the aortic cross clamp on, and started making my incision in the heart. Throughout the operation, I had to listen to the senior surgeon loudly criticizing my every move and every suture: "He just cut the coronary artery. It's all over. This patient is as good as dead. I cannot watch this mess anymore. I'm leaving. You might as well turn off the bypass machine!"

With singular concentration and sheer determination, I blocked these comments out of my conscious mind. There was a stunned, dead silence in the operating room except for the constant, loud, critical commentary. Finally, I com-pleted the repair successfully and closed the chest, and then I walked with the baby to the intensive care unit. When I was assured that the baby was stable and well, I went searching for the surgeon. A raging fury welled up in my chest. Although he was five inches taller and eighty pounds heavier than me, I was going to "kill" him for setting me up to fail and, more importantly, for placing a baby's life in imminent danger. I found him laughing with the other residents in the call room; they scattered when they saw me approaching. Words were exchanged over balled fists. Excuses were offered. Most of the conversation is unprintable.

The baby survived the surgery and recovered completely. I never forgot this lesson, though. Even today, I will never attempt an operation that I don't believe I can do successfully without the help of someone more experienced. I do not easily allow myself to be persuaded to do something that I am not completely comfortable doing. And I have never let a junior surgeon struggle in the operating room. No one ever needs to experience what I did that Tuesday afternoon in Cape Town.

19

The First Successful Neonatal Ebstein's Repair

In 1994 in Oklahoma City, I was walking past the neonatal intensive care unit (NICU) when I saw a lady weeping bitterly. She had long blonde hair, seemed to be in her thirties, and was very distraught. I approached her and asked if I could help her or get her a drink. She told me that her baby was dying in the NICU and that she was just waiting for the chaplain to arrive before the caretakers withdrew care because there was nothing they could do for the baby. She and her husband had been trying for years, unsuccessfully, to have a baby, and finally she had gotten pregnant. This was the last chance they would have, and her baby was going to die.

"I'm so sorry," I said. "What's wrong with your baby?"

"She has a fatal heart condition," she said.

I asked if she would like me to see her baby since I was a pediatric heart surgeon, and she prayerfully agreed. Well, the baby had a hitherto fatal condition called neonatal Ebstein's anomaly. She had severe heart failure, liver failure, jaundice, renal failure, and respiratory failure, and she was on a ventilator with low blood pressure. It looked dismal. Being the eternal optimist, thought, I told the mom that I had repaired a similar baby a few weeks ago and that the baby had survived, and I was prepared to try to repair her baby if she wanted me to. With some difficulty, I convinced the cardiologist to let me try to repair baby girl Knox. (When babies are born and are critically ill, they are often not assigned a name but rather are called "BG" for "baby girl" or "BB" for "baby boy," so this was BG Knox.) Well, the surgery was impossibly difficult and long, but BG Knox looked like she was going to survive and become the second baby ever to survive a complete repair of this condition.

That weekend, I brought my daughter Annie with me to do my rounds and showed her the still critically ill baby Knox. Annie was ten years old and saw the name BG on the door. Two weeks later, when Annie again rounded with me, I introduced her to baby Kayla Knox. "Is she related to BG Knox?" Annie innocently asked. "It's the same baby," I told her. "She is going home soon and her mommy and daddy, Kip and Crystal, have given her the name Kayla." Well, Kayla grew up into a beautiful young lady, participated in sports and ballet, and in 2017 at the age of twenty-three years, she required a second operation to replace the tricuspid valve that I had rebuilt more than two decades earlier.

20

In the Presence of Excellence

I've always felt that one should not accept that a problem is impossible to fix. One should rather challenge oneself to find a way to overcome what seems to be an impossible obstacle. And, in my own philosophy in surgery and in my lifestyle, one needs to simplify the problem, not clutter the mind with previous failures. One needs to have an open mind and prepare to change course in midstream in order to achieve these goals. This is how I approach the babies with Ebstein's anomaly.

In the case of babies with Ebstein's, the big problem is simplified into three smaller problems, which are each resolved separately. For instance, since the heart is too big for the chest, I make it smaller. Second, since the tricuspid valve is absent or very badly damaged, I repair it if I can or replace it if I can't. And finally, since the heart is too weak to pump the blood through the lungs, I support it until it's stronger, and then I minimize the resistance against which it needs to work. These are three smaller, fixable problems, rather than one big, insurmountable problem. This approach has resulted in numerous successful surgeries for babies with Ebstein's anomaly.

Surgery should be like poetry or classical music. Poetry is the music of language, a spoken symphony of sorts. Each word or phrase by itself is nothing, and yet, if it's properly strung together, it creates a perfect harmony that transcends understanding. And cardiac surgery should be a symphony of healing. One needs not only address the structural damage of the heart but also create a harmony among the body, mind, and spirit of the patient in order to succeed, especially in difficult cases. Probably the easiest way to explain it is that, as a surgeon, you need to imagine that you are the patient having surgery—that you're hungry, cold, scared, afraid to die, and hurting. And then, you need to address each of these aspects proactively. For example, if noise startles you, then you make sure that everybody whispers in the operating room and in the intensive care unit. If being cold makes you anxious, you need to make sure that everyone warms their hands before touching the patient. If the monitors, with all their bright lights and loud sounds, scare you, then you need to cover the patient's eyes so he or she can't see them and play gentle, soothing Mozart music to calm the patient, which is what I do. And then, if you're afraid of pain, then you need to ensure that you continuously prevent pain from occurring rather than reacting to the pain with pain killers when the patient cries. These are just a few examples of how you can make a horrific experience for an infant patient less traumatic physically and emotionally, not only for the patient but also for his or her family. We could extrapolate this to the whole world as a lovely philosophy.

We have many visitors in the operating room who come to watch an intricate cardiac operation on these tiny, little babies. They are in awe of the situation. As they lean over the drapes observing the surgery, I often tell them, tongue in cheek, "You are in the presence of excellence—never forget that!" But before they could acquiesce or stammer out a response, and with the chuckles from the rest of the team who have heard this joke many times before, I then add, "And I am slowly getting better too." It was a standard joke.

21

Converting a Starnes' Operation to a Biventricular Repair

Evyn Chilton was dying. Or rather, for all practical purposes, she was dead. Her mother, Kerri, was sitting in the cardiologist office waiting to sign the withdraw care order when she flipped open a cardiac surgery monthly publication and found the first report of successful neonatal repair of Ebstein's anomaly in eight babies in Oklahoma City. I had done these repairs in 1994 but had waited for five years before I published the results; I wanted to be sure that the repairs were successful and durable before I shared the remarkable success stories.

Stunned, she asked the cardiologist if he would contact me to see whether I was prepared to take on Evyn. Evyn had severe neonatal Ebstein's anomaly and had undergone a single ventricle palliation, called the Starnes operation. This converts the diseased heart into a single ventricle system, removing the septum that separates the heart into four chambers. But she was not doing well following the operation. After several weeks, she was still stuck on the ventilator (breathing machine) and still required a lot of support to keep her heart from stopping. After heroic efforts, she was dying, and Kerri had been advised that it was all over; it was time to remove the breathing tube, which was keeping her barely alive. She was finally ready to agree, until she read my article in the journal. The cardiologist had not read the article yet and was shocked when she read that the first few newborn babies with EA on whom I had operated had survived. She called me, and I told her I thought that I could convert Evyn's heart back into a normal heart with four chambers, even though this had never been done before. It would mean that I would have to take down the prior five-hour operation, rebuild the inside of the heart, and then repair the heart as I had done on the previous patients—a formidable task. And it would have to be undertaken in a baby who had been on the brink of death for several weeks.

Evyn was flown from Ochsner Clinic in New Orleans to Oklahoma City on a Friday night. She was kept on a ventilator and had several drips supporting her heart en route, as well as an experienced team of physicians accompanying her on the flight. Despite this, her tiny heart arrested several times during the flight, but the team somehow was able to restart it each time. She arrived late Friday night in very poor condition, so much so that I wondered whether taking her to the operating room was good or feasible. We went to the operating room very early on the Saturday morning.

I reopened her chest and placed her on the bypass machine with cannulas in her atrium and aorta. I cooled her down and divided and removed the Blalock-Taussig shunt. Then I clamped the aorta and arrested the heart with cardioplegia. I then opened the right atrium and cut out the patch over the tricuspid valve. The leaflets were scarred from the prior surgery, and I was not confident that I could use them to repair the valve. So I sewed in a bioprosthetic valve in the tricuspid position, taking care to avoid injuring the electrical system of the heart (conduction tissue that was very close to my suture lines). Next I septated the heart since the entire atrial septum had been resected during the Starnes repair. I replaced the septum with a patch of her pericardial sac, and I removed the aortic cross clamp to restart the heart. Amazingly, the heart started beating again, stronger and stronger. But I was not yet finished. I still had to address the pulmonary valve, which was obstructed and leaking. I replaced this valve with a pulmonary homograft that had been donated by a child who had died. Then we started some inotropic support and tried to see whether this tiny, mutilated heart was able to make a blood pressure consistent with survival. It did. In fact, it seemed to love having four chambers now instead of just the two it was used to having.

Eleven hours after we started the surgery, we wheeled Evyn back into the cardiac ICU. She looked great, other than the expected bleeding after such a long operation. But she recovered beautifully and got off the ventilator without much difficulty. For the first time in her life, she was able to breathe by herself. She made a full recovery and played normally like other kids. She went to school like other kids and was the valedictorian when she graduated from elementary school. Evyn has had her bioprosthetic valves changed out twice over the past eighteen years, but she remains a healthy, active teenager in 2018.

22

The Berlin Heart

It was a Tuesday in July 2006, and I had just taken over for Dr. Al Pacifico as the chief of pediatric cardiac surgery at the University of Alabama at Birmingham (UAB), the mecca of pediatric cardiac innovation and success under Dr. Pacifico and Dr. John Kirklin, and later his son, Dr. James Kirklin.

The phone rang. It was an emergency, the caller said in a voice that sounded agitated, breathless, and desperate. It was the pediatric cardiologist, and he was at the children's hospital in Birmingham. "What is your philosophy on patients that are coding?" he asked, referring to a situation in which a patient's heart has stopped.

"What do you mean?" I asked, puzzled.

"Well, in the past we would not consider placing a patient on ECMO (mechanical life-support system) if the patient was coding. But I wanted to know what your position is regarding this scenario. I have a seven-month-old baby here who arrested, and we have been doing chest compressions for about fifteen minutes already in another hospital."

"Have you stopped chest compressions at all? Do the pupils still react to light?" I asked.

"We have not stopped chest compressions, and I think the pupils are still reacting," he said.

"Bring her over. I'll put her on ECMO," I said. I assembled my team at the side of the fourth bed on the left side of the mixed adult/pediatric cardiac ICU. They wheeled in the infant some twenty-five minutes later, still actively doing chest compressions and ventilating the baby by hand. They had needed to move the baby into an ambulance and transfer her to my hospital and ICU. She had a viral myocarditis and dilated cardiomyopathy.

I expeditiously opened the right side of her neck and placed cannulas in the internal jugular vein and common carotid artery, taking care not to ligate these vessels in the process; this would give the baby a slightly better chance to recover normal brain function. We started the ECMO mechanical support and waited to see whether she would wake up and what neurological deficit would be present. Well, to everyone's amazement, she woke up the next day and appeared to have no significant brain injury. Even her heart function retuned, although the heart remained weak and unable to support her body. Dr. Jim Kirklin made some phone calls to the Berlin Heart company, and they brought a Berlin Heart to our hospital within thirty-six hours. That Friday, Dr. Kirklin and I placed the Berlin Heart in this baby, with the medical representative pretty much telling us how to do it as we went. This was possibly the first Berlin Heart to be placed in UAB. The Berlin Heart is the only ventricular assist device available for young infants in the United States and until then had only been used very infrequently in the country.

The infant survived the Berlin Heart operation and recovered very well. Although she suffered a few minor strokes during the next eighteen months or so, she remained well, although her own heart never recovered to the point that the Berlin Heart could be removed. Finally, Dr. Kirklin took the Berlin Heart out and did a successful heart transplant some eighteen months after the patient had coded and been placed on ECMO. At the time, she was the longest survivor on a Berlin Heart in the world. And she was a happy little toddler all through her trials and tribulations.

The lesson learned was that one needs to keep an "open philosophy" on patient care and that you never know it's all over until the fat lady has sung.

23

The History Lesson

Cardiac surgeons can be very pompous at times. That is a huge understatement. A wise, elderly cardiologist once said of cardiac surgeons, "They were frequently wrong but never in doubt." That kind of sums it up, I think (present company included).

However, I am a good, successful cardiac surgeon by most accounts. I love to teach, especially younger, trainee physicians, called fellows or residents. Most of the teaching I do occurs during cardiac intensive care ward rounds, which are daily at seven thirty in the morning.

Now, there are fast thinkers and slow thinkers. Fast thinkers use intuition, experience, and snapshot evaluations to instantaneously take in and process any given situation. Slow thinkers base their decisions on a more methodical, systematic approach to a problem. I am a fast thinker most of the time. I can look at a patient and in a couple of seconds decide whether the patient is very ill, is getting better, is well, or is out of danger. I can do this without a lot of data, which is collected, documented, recorded, and then presented by the fellows to the surgeons and intensivists during the ward rounds.

So when a fellow started presenting the collected data on a postoperative baby during ICU rounds, I quickly interrupted her. "Caitlin, all of that is a history lesson. I have no interest in all of that useless data. It's a reflection of what happened to the patient six to eight hours ago. I am only interested in the present. How is the patient doing now?" "Yes, sir," she replied, a little embarrassed. "The patient is fine, recovering well."

A little later during the same rounds on the same day, we were discussing another very sick little baby. Caitlin was presenting a very brief summary of the patient in accordance with my earlier request, when I interrupted her again. "Tell me—what are the blood results and the kidney and liver function results?" "Well, sir," she started, "a wise surgeon once told me that this data was superfluous, that it was just a history lesson." Then she added with a wry smile, "But since I love history and study history, I am happy to share this data with you."

Her commentary was appreciated by everyone on the rounds. Even I smiled and said, "Touché." And it was an example of the saying "What goes around comes around!"

24

The X-Ray Teaching Conference

Once a week at Oklahoma University Health Sciences Center, we had a teaching conference during which the chest x-rays of the patients who had undergone surgery were presented by the cardiothoracic surgery resident (trainee). It was a formal meeting that most faculty attended, including all the residents, fellows, interns, and nursing staff and some of the radiologists.

I was the self-proclaimed leader of the conference. I had a pretty good idea of how to read x-rays, and I was actually quite good at it. I emphasized the need for the residents to fully harness their powers of observation, to comprehensively look at the whole chest x-ray and not just the heart, adding that the chest x-ray could tell a whole story about the patient. I was on my pedestal and enjoying sharing my knowledge and experience with all those present. Well, Billy was the cardiothoracic fellow presenting the x-rays, and he was one of the very best fellows I had ever trained in more than twenty-five years. He was methodical and comprehensive in his approach. But not even Billy could escape my teaching points. "I want everyone in this room to look carefully at this chest x-ray," I began. "Billy says this patient had coronary bypass surgery, but that's not good enough. Look carefully, and the chest x-ray can tell you a complete story about the patient." I continued on my inflated pedestal. "If you look carefully at the x-ray, you can see that the patient is a woman—and a well-endowed woman, at that. Can you see the breasts on the x-ray, Billy? Why don't you start over and give us the full picture now." I sat down satisfied that I had scored some important points and I had shared my vast experience with the now silent, somewhat intimidated audience.

Billy took a deep breath. He seemed to be studying the x-ray carefully. He chose his next words very carefully as he started presenting the x-ray again. "I'm sorry, sir," he started. "This is a chest x-ray of an overweight man who ..." He never got to finish his sentence; he never smiled or made eye contact with anyone. But all the people in the room roared with laughter. I sat there sheepishly with a red face, knowing that I was no longer the undisputed leader of this conference—and that my reputation for teaching was at best a little shaky.

25

My South African Accent
Causing Trouble: Part 1

My South African accent is usually appreciated in the mid-South where I have practiced for the past twenty-six years. However, there are times when it has gotten me into trouble.

I was in the middle of a difficult cardiac, open-heart operation on a young child when a call came to the operating room from a nurse on the floor of the regular postoperative ward calling for help because the oxygen level had dropped alarmingly low on one of the little babies who had had surgery the previous week. This little baby was stable but still required supplemental oxygen via a cannula in his nose. The oxygen is delivered via an outlet in the wall; it passes through a bottle containing water to humidify the oxygen before being delivered to the baby. The registered nurse (RN), Emily, knew that I needed to be informed immediately if something bad was happening to my patients, and because I had little resources to help me at the time, she called in to the operating room and asked the person answering the phone to interrupt my surgery to tell me the problem.

Well, I was alarmed because little babies have very little reserve, and if their oxygen saturations drop below 85 percent or so (the normal is 92 to 95 percent) they may go into cardiac arrest. So I told my assistant in the operating room to watch the patient undergoing surgery while I ran to the ward to quickly check on Emily's baby. I was still scrubbed up in my operating room clothes as I ran past her into the baby's room. In a second, I realized that the humidifying bottle was not screwed into the wall properly, thus not delivering the required oxygen to the baby. It took but a second to screw the bottle tightly, and within seconds, the baby's oxygen levels had returned to normal. Satisfied, I ran back to the operating room. As I passed Emily on the way back to the operating room, I said to her, "You need to screw the bottle on!" She shrugged her shoulders indignantly and said, "I am going as fast as I can!" A little puzzled, I hesitated, returned, and asked her, "What did you think I just said to you?" "You said I need to scoot my butt along," she retorted angrily.

I was too busy to laugh then, but we all had a good laugh afterward.

26

My South African Accent Causing Trouble: Part 2

I had just started as the new chief of pediatric cardiac surgery at the University of Alabama in Birmingham, a position that became vacant when the great professor Al Pacifico retired. Dr. Pacifico's scrub nurses were assigned to me. They were the very best, most seasoned scrub nurses who had worked with the best in the world—Dr. Pacifico and Dr. John Kirklin, both giants in pediatric cardiac surgery. They were very well respected, soft spoken, and superefficient in the operating room. Dr. Pacifico did not tolerate talking or noise of any sort in the operating room. Scarla and Charlie, the scrub nurses, ruled the operating room and ensured that the environment was exactly the way their surgeon wanted it.

Charlie was in her midforties, a southern girl, a devout mother and wife, and a good Christian lady who never used colorful language or profanity of any kind. She wore glasses and was very quiet, polite, and well mannered. Well, we were in the middle of a long, difficult baby heart surgery when Charlie uncharacteristically handed me an incorrect suture. I looked up frankly surprised because she was so efficient and excellent at her job and noticed that her mask had loosened just a little under her eyes, allowing the exhaled breath to cloud her glasses. "You are a little fogged up, Charlie," I said understandingly. "Yes, sir," she replied. Not another word was spoken during the surgery, which was completed successfully.

After the surgery, I stopped into Connie Parten's office for a chat. Connie was the nurse manager of the cardiac ICU. "Charlie just left my office in tears," she said. "Said she has never been so humiliated in all her life. She made one small mistake during the surgery, and you said to her in front of all the staff that she was 'a little fucked up.'"

Needless to say, the confusion was quickly cleared up, and Charlie's glasses never got fogged up again. And if they had, I was not planning to comment on it!

27

Inauguration as a Fellow of American College of Surgeons

Being a fellow of the Fellow American College of Surgeons (FACS) is a big deal, especially to a farm boy from Africa working as an academic cardiac surgeon in America. It's a special honor bestowed upon only a few surgeons. If you are inducted as a fellow, you get to put "FACS" behind your name with all your other degrees. When I came to America in 1991, I personally knew only one surgeon with "FACS" behind his name—my chief in South Africa, Professor Pieter Barnard. Thus, when I was notified that I was being inducted into FACS, I was over the moon. I was also very conscious of the fact that this was a great honor for which I was to be very well prepared. I researched the ceremony and discovered that part of it involved singing the national anthem, the "Star-Spangled Banner."

Now, I knew the tune, but I did not know the words. I had very little time to learn them, and I certainly did not want to be disqualified at the ceremony because of that. However, I was also working a ninety-hour week and had a family with two children who needed my attention when I was not at the hospital. So I told my cardiac surgery resident, Debbie McCollum, that I would train her especially well with much patience if she would teach me the anthem while we were operating together. For about two to three weeks before I needed to leave for the ceremony, we sang the national anthem over and over in the operating room while doing coronary bypass surgeries or replacing cardiac valves. Well, neither of us had a particularly good voice or could hold a note properly, but we sang it again and again until I knew it and could repeat the words in song without falter. (We never sang during baby heart surgery—that would be unthinkable!) I was ready!

We arrived at the ceremony. My good friend, an esophageal surgeon from Ireland named Peter Crookes, and I sat together in the third row with all the other inductees, mostly prominent American surgeons. When it came time to sing the anthem, we were ready. Peter had a better singing voice than I, but he had a thick Irish accent. I had an enthusiastic, albeit audibly challenging, voice with a heavy South African accent. We sang together with passion and with the unstated realization that we were slightly out of our league but still being inducted as Fellows of the American College of Surgeons. However, after the second line, we also realized that we were the only two inductees who knew the words of the anthem—or the tune! So, the national anthem rang out loudly at this prestigious ceremony in the thick, unmistakable Irish and South African accents of the two proudest inductees present.

Twenty years later, I still remember the words of the "Star-Spangled Banner" and how I learned them with

Debbie McCollum in the operating room in Oklahoma City. And I'm still surprised to see how few sportsmen know these beautiful words when they play the anthem before football games or at the Olympics or other venues.

28

"Come On, Wind; Make Me Strong"

My running group and I had our two- to three-hour-long training runs at six thirty on Sunday mornings. A few of the members were Karrie, Donna, Joanne, Joe, Eva, Tiffany, Trey, Lane, Amos, Frank Willis, John, Bill, Little Bill, Sandra, and many others. I always ran in front, and if the wind was blowing in our faces, I would open my arms wide and challenge the wind to blow harder. A stronger headwind made it harder to run and thus built more stamina. Then we would all call out, "Come on, wind; make me strong."

Then, as we got closer to the end of the run and were exhausted, waiting to end the run, Amos would call out, "What did the rabbit say when they cut off his tail?" Then all of us would respond, "It won't be long now!"

29

My First Marathon Was a Nightmare

When you first consider running a marathon, it is hard to appreciate how difficult it is both physically and mentally. Adding additional individual challenges to this is preposterous, even delusional. Yet this is exactly what I did when I decided to run my first marathon.

Although I am not a natural or even a marginally adequate runner, I decided in the spring of 2000 to run a marathon and either finish the marathon or die in the process. At least, this is what I told everyone! Running a marathon (26.2 miles, or 42 kilometers) had been a lifelong goal to which I had aspired but not achieved. I had occasionally run two or three miles and most often collapsed afterward on the driveway of my Edmond home, with my kids hosing me down with water and wondering whether or not they needed to call an ambulance. But I wanted to run a marathon and, thus, started training. Then I went on public record as saying that I was not a quitter (which is true!) and that I would finish the marathon or die trying.

My running buddy was a cardiologist, George Kumar. We did our long runs around Lake Hefner together and even ran a half marathon together in Norman, Oklahoma. Together, we entered the inaugural Oklahoma City Memorial Marathon, which was held on April 29, 2001. I read Hal Higdon's "Marathon" handbook religiously each evening, studied the course topography, and did all my homework for the race. This was going to be a family affair, and my children, Chris and Annie, and my then wife, Danese, were all excited and supportive yet filled with trepidation.

The night before the marathon was prom night in Edmond, and it was unusually chaotic. We went out to a local Italian restaurant for our pasta meal and had to wait until all the prom couples had left before we could be seated and served, which was after nine thirty in the evening. I had my customary Guinness draft beer and a seafood pasta meal. George and I had agreed to meet at six thirty the next morning, a half hour before the marathon was set to start in downtown Oklahoma City. Well, we arrived home and I went to bed with my running shoes and clothes carefully arranged on the chair in front of my bed. My running number was pinned to my shirt, and my time chip was secured to my shoelace. I was so ready! However, I awoke just after midnight with projectile vomiting and a fever, and I continued to vomit and have diarrhea every ten minutes for the rest of the night. I had contracted food poisoning during dinner. I sat in front of the toilet bowl the entire night with either my face or my behind in the bowl until a quarter to six in the morning. At that point, I was exhausted; still feverish, though less so than earlier; and still hoping to run. Against objections from my family, I donned my clothes and planned at least to capture the excitement of the start of the marathon for which I had trained so hard. I hoped to run a few miles with my running buddy just for fun and to support him.

At the start line, the atmosphere was exhilarating, though somber at the same time. The memories of the victims of the Murrah Building bombing massacre were honored. Then the runners were given a pep talk, the national anthem was sung, the gun was fired, and we were off. My first marathon had started.

George and I had planned to run a four-hour marathon (another somewhat unrealistic goal for a first marathon), but by the time I had reached the one-mile marker, I was breathing hard and my legs felt like jelly. I was sweating profusely and could not keep any fluid down—either I vomited or had diarrhea or both. I waved George on and looked for the mobile toilets every half mile or so. By mile four, I had used the mobile toilets seven times for diarrhea, and I could not keep any fluids in my body for more than a few minutes. My stomach and back muscles were aching from retching the previous night, and I was in agony. I looked through blurred eyes for my wife to take me home, less humiliated than devastated by my misfortune. I finally saw Danese at mile six, at which point I was mostly walking and jogging intermittently, and I felt terrible! When Danese saw me, she wouldn't listen. She kept encouraging me to go on, saying I was looking good, I was tough, and I was a fighter. Even as I pleaded for her to take me home, she persistently urged me: "Just a few miles more. I'll take you home at the ten-mile mark if you're still sick."

So, on and on I went, walking, jogging, and standing for a while. I had long since quit enjoying the marathon. I had quit thinking about my promise to finish; I had quit looking for a toilet. The diarrhea now just ran down my legs, unguarded, down into my socks. At mile ten, I could not find Danese. I could not find anyone I knew to take me home, and

I was too delirious or stupid to look for the medical truck. I found a portable toilet at mile eleven and hid in it, resolving that I would hide there until the marathon was over and Danese could come and find me. I remember sitting and shivering on the toilet, hoping to die so the pain in my joints would stop. It was agony even to stand up. My back muscles felt like they had all been torn and were having spasms continuously. Angry banging on the toilet door forced me to give up my refuge and keep moving on.

At mile twelve, my dear friend Dr. Nazir Zuhdi was waiting to cheer me on. We had had dinner together with our wives a few days earlier at La Bougette. Dr. Zuhdi, head of the Zuhdi Institute and one of the greatest pioneer cardiac surgeons, had promised to wait for me at this point to cheer me on. As I approached our rendezvous spot, I was barely walking and had watery diarrhea trickling down my legs. Looking and feeling like death, I spotted Nazir leaning against the railing of a parking lot on the left side of Britton Road. At first, my heart cried out with relief; he would understand. He would see how totally finished I was and would take me home, safely home. Then I noticed that he had nodded off, probably from waiting for me for so long. So I tiptoed past him, praying now that he would not wake up and see me or recognize the South African T-shirt in which I was running. I imperceptibly moved past him and past the half-marathon point, gaining a little comfort from the fact that I would later jokingly admonish him for falling asleep when I needed him the most.

On and on I moved, not running, along the Lake Hefner bicycle path. There, I ultimately collapsed, lying face down on the tarmac ground, crying like a baby. As I lay sobbing, unable to lift my head or my body, another runner stopped and helped me up. He encouraged me to go on and gave me two Advil pills that he had in his running shorts. I did go on again, looking desperately for a familiar face. I knew that Danese, who knew how sick I had been the previous night, would recognize that this was madness, tell everyone that I had put up a valiant fight, and force me to retire. She would encourage me to do another marathon when I was healthy. I found her at last, just before mile fourteen. She was enthusiastic that I had finished more than half the marathon. She asked if I could try for just one more mile, saying that our good friends, Ursula and George Pahl, were waiting there, and they had a car there and could take me home. Plus, they would be so disappointed if they did not see me.

I had no strength to argue. I had this fatalistic attitude now, almost an out-of-body experience. My pain consumed me to the extent that I was numb all over. I sucked on a piece of candy she gave me. I had still not drunk anything, but at least the diarrhea and vomiting had now stopped. However, my body was on fire. I could not hold my arms up to run, I could not bend my elbows to run, my back felt like it was tearing off my body, and my knees felt like nails were being driven through the joints. I had unbelievable pain! I knew that if I stopped moving, I would not start again. My son was less than a mile ahead with the Pahl family and the car.

I finally found Chris. I grabbed onto him and told him that I was dying, that he needed to get me to the hospital immediately. "Come on, Dad," he said. "I'll run with you a while." Chris had on flip-flops—unfit for running. I stopped and cried and ran and cried. No one would listen to me. He said the car was just ahead and that he would take me home when we reached it, but we never seemed to reach it. At last he pointed and said, "There!"

We were now at mile sixteen, and my daughter and the Pahls were at the side of the road with snacks, drinks, and banners with cheerful slogans, and they had big, happy faces! I tried to straighten my back a little and smile through glazed eyes and my pain. I remember Ursula Pahl saying to me, "Oh, my God, Chris, come here! Oh, my God! You don't have to do this anymore." But my daughter was now with me, looking into my eyes with pride and admiration. I couldn't stop then, not in front of her. "I'll run with you, Dad," she said, taking my hand. Through my oblivion, I realized that I needed to cool down. Since I could not drink, I poured water over my head and body. The first time was to wash the diarrhea off my clothes and legs, but I sensed that this was good for me, so I did it every half mile or so. I sipped some water, which I did not throw back up. Ursula had some ice cubes, and I placed some under the cap on my head to cool me down; I sucked on some too. I continued with my daughter, walking and jogging. She talked to me the whole time, telling me stories of when they were little, things we had done together as a family, what a good example I was to her, and how she admired me. Soon, we passed the nineteen-mile mark. Then, for the first time, I thought that maybe, just maybe, I could hold on till the end; maybe I could indeed finish the marathon.

Now, I struggled to focus my eyes, struggled to see. Annie took my hand and walked and ran with me, holding my hand all the way. She was sixteen years old and had never jogged before in her life, but she held my hand, and I could not let her down. She was so brave, so determined that I was not going to let myself down by not finishing; she would help me. She kept talking. At mile twenty-two, after pulling me and leading me for six miles, she fell silent from fatigue. Then I started talking to her. "Come on, Princess," I said. "We're almost there. I can't see where I am going. You need to show me the way." Before I realized it, Danese and my son Chris were also there beside me as we passed the twenty-five-mile marker. Now I was stronger. I felt no pain anymore. In fact, I could not feel anything and could not even see anything except blurred images. But I felt okay; my mind was strong again.

Suddenly, we were on Broadway Avenue at Tenth Street, five hundred yards from the finish line. We all held hands, the whole family, and we ran, laughed, and cried together as we waved at the crowds—Danese, carrying all the clothes and discarded garments; Annie, with a very pale face and drawn lips after jogging more than ten miles with me; and Chris, with his blistered feet and flip-flops and big, beautiful smile. We crossed the finish line together, a triumphant family. The official clock said five hours and thirty-four minutes, more than one hour and forty minutes after my running buddy, George, had finished. The second split was three hours and twenty minutes!

At the finish line was Nathan Dilley, an emergency medical technician at Children's Hospital. We knew each other and had taken care of sick babies together many times. He was a medical volunteer at the finish line. I vaguely remember him taking me from the finish line and going inside the triage center. Within minutes, he and Dr. Tom Coniglione, the medical director of the marathon and a marathoner himself, were frantically pumping IV fluids into both of my arms simultaneously. From dehydration, my kidneys had shut down, and the arteries to my eyes had undergone spasms— that was the reason I couldn't see. After four liters of IV fluids in ten minutes, I eventually started shivering, which was a good sign—a sign that I should survive the experience. Much later, I was allowed to go home; I insisted. It took eighteen hours of constantly drinking fluids before I could pass urine, and another day before I could see properly. But I eventually recovered, primarily due to the efforts and vigilance of these two colleagues.

So, you may ask, "Did your first marathon live up to its reputation as a major physical and mental feat?" You better believe it! But it was more than four months before I could bring myself to lace up my sneakers and run again.

I have continued running marathons, though, and my closet is filled with commemorative T-shirts from the various races. The following year, I ran the Second Memorial marathon in three hours and forty-three minutes, almost two hours faster than my first marathon. Subsequently, I have run seven consecutive marathons, each in under four hours. To this day, however, I have never worn my finisher's T-shirt from my first marathon; it just doesn't seem right for me to wear it without the rest of my family wearing it with me.

My first marathon changed my approach to running; it fostered a greater love and respect for the sport. I am mentally much stronger as a result of it. I don't make predictions anymore, and I always look to help struggling runners during marathons, like my family and friends helped me. I will never again underestimate the resolve needed to complete a first marathon. I look out for fellow marathoners and hang out with them, proud to be included as their friend, as one of them—a marathoner too—because now I know and have experienced firsthand the agony of the first marathon.

30

Spiritually Based Utterances and Statements

I have always enjoyed reading books with assortments of quotations and idioms. Over the years I have accumulated and contributed several favorite quotations, some of which are listed below.

"You never get tired of helping someone who is in real need."

"Prayer is not talking to God but listening to Him."

"Adversity is the fundamental building block of inner strength."

"When it's noisy, you cannot hear God."

"A gentle touch has more healing power than most medicines."

"You never tire of doing something you like—enjoy life."

31

Miracles in Medicine

People often ask me if I have witnessed any miracles in my profession. I usually reply, "Do you mean this month?" But it's a sensitive topic, especially with the skepticism and rationalization prevalent in today's society. However, I have witnessed miracles in my practice of cardiac surgery—and more than once too. The following story is such an example.

In 1996, I was operating on a newborn baby with a condition called truncus arteriosus, a complicated congenital heart lesion with which we had previously experienced disappointing results. I was both nervous and particularly determined to have a good outcome this time, and I prayed hard as I scrubbed up before the start of the surgery. The surgery went well, and after about three hours, I separated the baby from the cardiopulmonary bypass machine, which maintains the circulation while the heart is being repaired. The baby's heart looked fantastic; it required minimal support to maintain a good blood pressure. All that was left was to dry up the chest (ensure that there was no important bleeding before closing the chest). Being extra cautious, I persisted in checking and rechecking the suture lines to make extra sure that there was no bleeding. I felt elated! I remember thinking that I had this heart condition licked and need not fear it again. Boy, I was good! I sent word out to the family that the baby was fine and that I would be out to visit with them shortly.

The bypass machine was being disassembled, and the perfusionist was cleaning up while I was getting ready to close the chest. It was around noon. The last thing I did before closing the chest was to cauterize a little bleeding spot on the aorta close to my suture line. Well, the electrocautery inadvertently melted the suture on the aorta, resulting in a sudden and uncontrollable massive hemorrhage. Within minutes, the baby had exsanguinated herself onto the floor, despite our valiant efforts both to control the bleeding and replace the blood loss. The only means to save her was by using the bypass machine, which had been disassembled and would require at least fifteen minutes to reassemble. In a heartbeat, it was all over! All the planning, the hundreds of sutures meticulously placed, the emotional torment and anguish of the preparation and surgery itself—it was all wasted, completely wasted. Now, the heart lay empty and limp in my hands. At this point, with a sobbing heart and naked of all pretense, I stopped. I closed my eyes and prayed once more, "Almighty God, I have failed You, again. I wanted so badly for this baby to survive, not so much to honor You through my work but rather to show others what a good surgeon I am. Now I know that there is nothing more I can do for this child; I know it and everyone in this operating room knows it. But, You, O God, have the power to heal and to save this little one. Forgive me my arrogance and save this baby, not for my sake but because You are a merciful and loving God." We rapidly reassembled the bypass machine, connected the baby to it, and redid the aortic suture line. Throughout the remainder of the surgery, there was a shocked quietness in the operating room. Not a whisper could be heard, no orders were spoken out loud, and everyone seemed to know what was needed. There was a peace not experienced before. Time was suspended, and the presence of God in the operating room was evident to all, even the anesthesiologist, an agnostic. We completed the surgery without the need for a single additional suture, and there was no bleeding afterward at all. I left the operating room at about four thirty that afternoon to visit with the family. I told them all that had happened and emphasized that without the divine intervention of the Lord, there was no chance that their baby would ever wake up from the operation. Then I locked myself in the bathroom and cried— truly sobbed. I knew then how the prodigal son must have felt when he returned and spoke with his father. I felt small, humble, and privileged to be an instrument to glorify God. I did not feel like a great surgeon at all, and I still don't.

I thought that the baby would be neurologically devastated. However, she recovered rapidly and without complications, and she was neurologically completely normal. She was a happy and contented little baby and then child, and now she's an adult. I learned a tough spiritual lesson, but everyone in the operating room that day learned that God is alive and waiting to be called upon.

This child is now a healthy twenty-one-year-old adult wanting to start a family of her own.

32

The Miracle Coronary Bypass Operation

I was excited to be asked to be the first assistant for a special coronary bypass operation on my professor of forensic pathology while I was in medical school. I liked him, and we all thought he was a great teacher and celebrity. He needed a quadruple coronary bypass operation. Dr. Lubbe was the surgeon, and I was the assistant for this private practice operation at Tygerberg Hospital in 1986.

The surgery went well; there were no problems, and it was a good repair. But at the end of the operation, the heart would not start back up and could not make any blood pressure. "Just needs a little time to recover," said Dr. Lubbe. Well, we gave it more time, lots and lots of more time. We also gave lots of drugs to help it make a blood pressure: dopamine, dobutamine, epinephrine, and so on. Nothing worked. My favorite professor's heart would not work and would not make a blood pressure compatible with life. This was before ventricular assist devices (VADs) and other methods currently used today. Things became frantic in the operating room, with a lot of finger-pointing and cursing.

Finally, four hours later, Dr. Lubbe announced that it was all over, that there was no hope or chance of survival. He left me in the operating room with the patient still on cardio-pulmonary bypass and went out to tell the family that the patient would not survive so he was turning off the bypass machine and letting nature take its course. He was letting him die.

Dr. Lubbe stayed away for about an hour. During that time, I remembered that Dimitri Nowitzki, a heart transplant surgeon who worked with Professor Christiaan Barnard, had used thyroxine for intractable heart failure. "Let's give him some intravenous thyroxine," I suggested to the anesthesiologist. "No, man, Dr. Lubbe will kill me. He is just looking for an excuse for this patient's death," he responded. "I'll say I did it. Give him an ampule," I said. I prayed long and hard with my eyes closed, standing over the patient who was all but dead—my favorite professor.

Suddenly, within ten to fifteen minutes of administering the drug, the miracle happened. The heart started squeezing better and better. The blood pressure got better and better. After a while, I turned off the bypass machine, and the heart took over and was working great. Unbelievable! Well, by the time Dr. Lubbe returned to the operating room, the patient was off the bypass machine, most of the drips and drugs had been weaned and discontinued, and my favorite professor was looking great. He was going to live!

"What happened?" Dr. Lubbe asked incredulously. At first I was too embarrassed to say that I had prayed *and* given thyroxine. I later shared these facts with him. Dr. Lubbe left the operating room for the second time, this time to tell the family that their loved one had miraculously recovered.

My favorite professor recovered uneventfully and returned to a normal life without complications. To this day, I don't believe he ever knew how close he came to dying or that divine intervention was instrumental in thwarting this outcome. I know I never told him.

And I never mentioned thyroxine either, although I have used it several times since then.

33

Now *That* Is What You Call Commitment

A complicated cardiac operation was in progress at the Veterans Affairs hospital in Oklahoma City. Dr. Elkins was the chief of cardiac surgery and was helping perform a double-valve replacement on an elderly man. The surgery was long and not going well. Debbie McCollum was the chief resident and was primarily doing the operation. As the operation progressed and the wheels kept coming off, Dr. Elkins assumed the lead surgeon role. Debbie was heavily pregnant at the time, but this was a forgotten detail as the surgery unraveled and the situation became critically unstable.

Some seven hours into the operation, Dr. Elkins called me to the operating room to help. The aorta was falling apart, and the patient was exsanguinating in front of our eyes. The second assistant, Joy, by this time, had scrubbed out and left the hospital in accordance with the VA hospital's requirements. Dr. Elkins had a meeting he needed to attend, and so he also left the building. He asked me to take over (and possibly sign the death certificate). Well, I placed the patient back on the bypass machine and replaced the aortic root with a homograft root, a complicated operation when done de novo and a heroic undertaking under these circumstances. Debbie and I worked hard for another three hours until we had the heart fully rebuilt, and we came off bypass without difficulty and with very little bleeding. Debbie never complained as we worked side by side until the end when we were closing the chest.

At that point, my foot slipped on something wet on the floor of the operating room. Thinking it was probably blood from the patient, I initially ignored it, but when I slipped again, I looked down and saw the floor was covered with fluid. Alarmed, I looked up at Debbie and asked, "Did you just pee on the floor? I'm so sorry. I should have let you have a bathroom break!" "No, sir," she replied. "My water broke during the operation. I think I am in labor!" "You're kidding me," I said. "Get the hell out of here, and get to the hospital!"

"No, sir. Thank you for saving his life. I can close the patient, sir," she replied.

"Get out," I ordered her. She had been operating for two hours with her water broken, never saying a word because she realized that I could not finish the operation without an assistant.

I thought, *Now* that *is commitment and determination!*

And she had a normal, healthy baby very soon thereafter.

34

The Cardiac Surgery
Christmas Party in 1987

Traditions, cultural practices, and preconceived convictions are difficult to change, especially in a threatened community like Israel or white South Africa in the mid-1980s. I completed my training as a cardiac surgeon in Cape Town in 1986 and became a consultant cardiac surgeon at Tygerberg Hospital, which was the hospital affiliated with the University of Stellenbosch, in January 1987.

At the end of that year, tradition dictated that we have a Christmas party in December (summertime in South Africa). As the new faculty member, I was to organize it. Previously, only the white staff were invited or encouraged to attend these parties, such as the white physicians, white nurses, white perfusionists, and white administrators.

This year, I wanted everyone to attend—the whole team. At that time, apartheid was still the norm in South Africa. Nelson Mandela was still in prison on Robben Island. Toilet facilities were still segregated, as were restaurants and other public places. Although many of my colleagues thought it was an okay idea to have an integrated party, not everyone did. Furthermore, it was difficult to find any establishment or venue prepared to risk an evening of food and alcohol in a multiracial environment. So I decided to have the party at my home instead. (I was always somewhat of a rebel, I suppose.)

We invited everyone! I sponsored the wine, beer, and the lamb, which we were to grill outside over open fires, as was the custom—a *braaivleis*. It was heartwarming to see the excitement among the nonwhite nursing staff. This was very new for them too. Even though we worked together, their significant others were, in many respects, less refined than them and less used to mingling with white people socially, and they were not at all used to sharing toilets or wash basins, or anything, really. Colored and black nurses and perfusionists all came to the party; it was the first time they had been invited to a white celebration. Several of the white cardiac surgeons "could not make it," but the evening was well attended.

Most of my white colleagues left perfunctorily at eleven at night, as was polite. But once they had left, the real party started with the nonwhite colleagues. My wife and I insisted on waiting on them hand and foot and told them that they had worked very hard the whole year serving us, so this was our opportunity to serve them for one night.

The evening was a wonderful success, eventually. But it was not without its problems. The whites did not want to use the same bathrooms that the nonwhites used; and neither wanted to use plates or cutlery used by people of the other races, either. As the wine and beer flowed, and social filters were removed, a little interracial belligerence surfaced and was frantically contained by those with the most to lose— the black or mixed-race nursing staff, who cussed out their husbands and boyfriends in no uncertain terms. The same husbands and boyfriends, being confronted with free beer and wine and food probably for the first time in their lives, started carrying stashes away and hiding it in their cars.

When the dust settled, it was a great evening notwithstanding all the hiccups and concerns. When the white colleagues had all left around eleven o'clock and the boisterous nonwhite husbands and significant others had been shooed home, the core of kindhearted souls remained—whites and blacks and mixed-race people, which included staff nurse Solly, staff nurse Johnson, and Sister Mossie, who had longed to share an evening together, and then the party really started. We laughed and joked and ate and retold stories until four thirty Sunday morning.

When we woke up the next day, our home was a mess. But it was worth it. Everyone felt good about the fact that we had just had the first multiracial party in the history of the department, and maybe even the country. So my wife and I started cleaning up the mess.

Around eleven o'clock, we heard a knock at the door. Staff nurse Johnson was there with her two daughters, aged around nine and eleven. She brought with her a bowl of flowers to thank my wife and me for hosting the party and including them. She also brought a handful of dollar bills to help compensate us for the wine and beer that had been carried away by the nonwhite husbands; the blacks who had come had collected some money at the end of the party to apologize and compensate us. (Naturally, we acknowledged but did not accept this gesture.) She and her daughters came to help clean up our home. It meant so much to me, this small gesture.

No one else came to help clean up, but then I didn't

expect them to. However, staff nurse Johnson and her lovely kids in their Sunday best clothes working with me to clean up made it all worthwhile. Later, they stood in front of their mom and me with their hands clutched tightly in front of their tummies, shaking their heads vigorously from side to side. When I asked them if they wanted some Kool-Aid to drink, my heart broke again. I realized that although they were thirsty, they had been told not to drink anything so that they would not need to use our toilets out of respect for us. The gratitude in their eyes and in their mother's eyes when I showed them to the bathroom and brought them something cool to drink on that hot summer's day is something I'll not easily forget.

With a long sigh, I realized how much we take for granted being white and how little we know, or care to know, about the struggle of people to be dignified and accepted as integrated citizens because they have dark skin or speak with a country accent. How little things have changed deep down in our hearts twenty-five years later.

35

"These Facts, If True"

These words were uttered by a great cardiac pathologist at Boston Children's Hospital, Professor Richard van Praagh. He was discussing the number of leaflets of the truncal valve in the condition truncus arteriosus. "There may be two, three, or four leaflets," he said. "I had a patient who had five leaflets," I said, wanting to be recognized and feel important. He never told me I was mistaken, but he looked up at the ceiling, put a finger on his chin, and said, "Ah, now Chris, these facts, if true, would be astonishing."

36

Achievement Is Addictive

There is something about achievement and success that is so addictive, so contagious, and so exhilarating. Have you ever noticed the heightened tone of your voice, the renewed spring in your step, and the almost breathless excitement you experience when you successfully complete a difficult task? It could be an intellectual task, a fine-motor exercise, a physically demanding routine, or even singing a difficult song.

Take two people running a marathon, for instance—equally competent athletes in all respects. Both complete twenty-six miles when one trips, sprains an ankle, and is unable to complete the race while the other safely crosses the finish line. The first runner is physically exhausted, inconsolably dejected, and emotionally devastated. The other runner strides around euphoric, indomitable, and elated. Both are equally tired, and both have endogenous endorphins pulsing through their veins, yet, achievement has rendered them different, totally distinct physically, emotionally and spiritually. Amazing!

Consider a musician who has just completed faultlessly

playing a challenging piece of classical music. The person glows, cannot stop grinning, bounces around the concert hall like a wound-up toy, speaks a hundred miles per hour, and may even be incorrigible. Contrast this with a musician who, having practiced equally hard, slept equally little preparing for the performance, and is equally nervous, messes up while playing the same piece. This musician's face is drawn and seems to have aged perceptibly. He is sullen, has no desire to talk, and seems ready to curl up in the fetal position. Both had adrenaline pumping and hearts racing when they started playing. What changed? What is the difference between them other than success?

The same is true for someone putting the finishing touches to an especially well-written essay or article; taking a critical test and knowing he or she has excelled; completing a difficult surgery successfully; or preparing a special meal that looks and tastes fantastic. The adulation, admiration, and respect of colleagues, family, or friends unquestionably contributes to this euphoria—no doubt about that! But it is not central to it. For even when we are completely alone and achieve success, we experience the same feelings physically, emotionally, and spiritually. Take, for instance, the uninhibited antics of the mountaineer who finally reaches the summit and is alone; the student who has been grappling with an impossible mathematical problem and then solves it alone; or that soprano hitting a perfect pitch for the first time while practicing alone.

No, achievement is an integral part of our genetic makeup. It is as necessary for our well-being as food and water. Achievement and success are what drive us to be better than we were yesterday. It is what makes yesterday's heroes forgotten and today's heroes temporary. Achievement is the personification of "survival of the fittest"; it is the driving force to be the best, to reach our potential, and to multiply our talents. Achievement nurtures our very nature and our inherent, undeniable desire to find our God and be more like Him.

37

An Act of Civil Duty

September 11, 2001, affected everyone to a larger or smaller degree, even me—actually, especially me. I remember standing in the cardiac intensive care unit (CICU) of Children's Hospital in Oklahoma City and berating the nursing staff for not paying closer attention to my patient who had undergone a Norwood operation, a very complicated cardiac operation done on newborn babies, the previous day. Unable to get their attention, I glanced over their shoulders to see what was on the TV that intrigued them enough to disregard my sick baby and saw the second plane fly right into the World Trade Center. I almost threw up.

The aftermath was an equally difficult time. Everyone was on edge. All citizens developed a heightened sense of vigilance, and everyone wanted to help prevent the next disaster, including me. I was a cardiac surgeon and had received some national attention for innovative cardiac operations I had successfully done on little babies. The community had embraced this, and I felt a bit like a local hero, albeit a very busy, very tired, rather disorganized, and mostly-late-for-everything local hero.

I raced from the operating room to my car and drove to Edmond Memorial High School, home of the Bulldogs, to see my son perform in the marching band. I was late as usual. My wife and my family had come to expect this by now: "Dad's saving lives; he'll be here soon ... I think." So I double-parked my car in a disabled space at the school grounds and ran across the adjoining field to where the crowd of always-on-time parents and families were waiting. I approached the crowd from the back, hoping to join in and fake having arrived earlier. I pushed my way through the crowd toward the front, knowing that my son, who was down on the field below, would be scouring the crowd for signs of his father. Needless to say, I was in a state of agitation, hypoglycemic from operating and not eating, and sweaty.

As I got to the front row of the spectators on the terrace above the field where the band was to perform, an incredibly loud *boom* rang out. It almost burst my eardrums, and it scared the bejesus out of me. A bomb! A terrorist had detonated a bomb within ten or fifteen feet of me. In a split second, my instincts took over, and I grabbed the woman next to me, threw her to the ground, and covered her with my whole body to protect her from the blast. She was a young mother in a summer dress, also there to support the marching band or the cheerleaders or a neighbor's child or something. I had saved her!

She was clearly startled, her dress up around her head now as she lay under my protective body right in the midst of hundreds of other spectators who would perish from this bomb attack. But I had managed to save this one woman.

She did not move beneath my body. A few seconds later, I noticed that all the other spectators around us were not dead; in fact, they not only had miraculously survived the blast, but they were staring at us in a curious way. Then the band started playing below where we lay on the grass. My instincts again kicked in as I realized that the "blast" was caused not by a bomb but by the single beat of the bass drum of the band, which was located just in front of the person I was trying to get past to see the band when I arrived. This was the signal for the band to start playing.

I quickly got up off the ground and mumbled, "Sorry," as I helped the startled and shocked woman to her feet. I tried to explain that I thought it had been a bomb, but the words and sentences didn't seem to come out right in my South African accent. The crowd around us had not moved. No one said a word. They just stared at me, and now it was I who felt like the terrorist from whom I had tried to protect her. Then I said, "Oh, shit!" and walked away and back to my car across the field, still in a state of shock and self-consciousness, fully expecting to be arrested and carted off to jail.

I never saw the band perform that day. I never saw the rest of my family that day, and I never saw that poor woman ever again. At subsequent band performances, I always looked around discreetly to see if I could somehow recognize her to properly apologize, but I never did. The experience was traumatic enough that I totally blocked out her face from my conscious recollection. I often wondered what she said after I left or when she got home that day after being wrestled to the ground by a stranger in the midst of family and friends and hundreds of other spectators, with her dress up around her head on a hot summer's afternoon in Oklahoma City.

38

Favorite African Proverbs

The stars shine more brightly when the moon is not full.

Never test the depth of the river with both feet.

39

The Bushman Arrows

Given to Christopher J. Knott-Craig, MD, FACS, in 1979 by a father of an infant he treated in Botswana/Namibia. The father was a Vasquela Bushman (yellow pigmy race, indigent to southern Africa). Presented to Dr. Nazih Zuhdi on May 19, 2006, by Dr. Knott-Craig in recognition of his friendship, mentorship, and spiritual brotherhood.

I was stationed on the front lines during the war between Angola and South Africa in 1979. I was a full lieutenant in the medical corps of the South African Army as part of my two-year compulsory military service. My group attended to the medical needs of the armed forces and the indigent people and their families. The indigents belonged to the Bushman race, best known for their amazing tracking skills. The tribal custom dictated that if a family member died in the hut (home), the hut had to be burned to the ground and a new one built to replace it. For that reason, a sick infant was often treated by the tribal medicine man or witch doctor, or *sangorma,* until death was imminent, at which time the father would run, carrying the baby, to the gazebo hospital and deposit the gasping child in the hospital, where death would very soon occur, usually within hours. On one such day, I looked at a gasping infant dying of gastroenteritis and dehydration before my eyes. In desperation, I stuck an adult IV into the baby's abdomen and ran in IV fluids, and amazingly, the infant recovered. When the father came back to the hospital two days later and saw his healthy baby, he was overwhelmed with joy and insisted on giving to me his bow and all five of his arrows—his entire means to fend for and provide for his family until he could make a bow and arrows again. So great was his love for his baby and so great was his gratitude to me for saving his baby's life.

In 1990, I presented one of the five arrows to Dr. Aldo Casteneda in Cape Town, the chief of pediatric cardiac surgery at Boston Children's Hospital at the time. He was an international giant in congenital heart surgery and a mentor of mine.

Dr. Nazi Zuhdi was also a giant in the development of cardiac surgery as it is practiced today. He has been a friend to me for twenty-five years and a mentor and confidante for just as long. He died in 2017 in Oklahoma City. It was with admiration and appreciation for his services to patients with heart disease that I presented one of these arrows to him in 2006 when he hosted a farewell party for me at his country club. The remaining three arrows are still in my possession. The arrow presented to Dr. Zuhdi is the only other genuine Bushman's arrow in the United States.

40

Hospital Care Is Different from Hospital Caring

Time spent in the hospital is usually very traumatic and often frustrating for the families of infants and children having major surgery. Once the critical period has passed and the family is assured that the surgery was successful and the child is going to be all right, that is when the frustration and irritation really start to kick in. This period of convalescence for the parents and families is equally demanding of caregivers' understanding and appreciation as the initial few days after surgery when everyone is just happy that things are going to be okay. Physicians and nursing staff need to be just as diligent in recognizing and ameliorating these concerns.

After the birth of our baby Catherine Rae in 2016, we experienced some of these same frustrations firsthand. It seemed like every time my wife would fall asleep following her C-section, someone would come in the room to check her vital signs, wake her up to give pain medicine, or ask her a seemingly irrelevant question. Although everyone was very friendly and happy that all was well, they had no idea that someone else had entered our room twenty minutes earlier for some other reason. As soon as our baby fell asleep and we finally settled down to quickly get some synchronized rest, another nurse would come into the room to check Cate's vital signs, to check whether she was feeding okay, to make sure we had ordered lunch, to see whether we wanted to get newborn baby pictures taken, to clean the room, to take out the previous untouched meal, or to just come in to check on us. When they entered, they spoke in a normal but loud voice, and invariably, when they left, the door would loudly bang closed.

It drove us crazy! As a physician and a nurse, we understood that everyone was doing his or her job, but no one seemed to have any understanding that there were fifteen other people also doing their jobs. As a result, I was rapidly getting ticked off, my wife was getting ticked off, and Baby Cate was getting *very* ticked off. There's a name for this type of frustration: it's called sleep deprivation. (Anyone know what I'm talking about?)

With the treating team on board, we introduced my solution: each time my wife and baby finally got to sleep at the same time, I put up a notice on the outside of the door that said, "Mother and baby fell asleep at 12:15 p.m. Do not wake them before 4:30 p.m." I left out the "for fear of your own safety" part.

So let us analyze for a moment the genesis of this frustration and how we address it in order to provide "hospital caring" and not just "hospital care."

Parents and family all understand that a hospital stay is needed to ensure the health and safe recuperation of the patient. For this to occur, certain things need to be done: medications have to be given on time, patient's vital signs need to be monitored, and so on. However, all nursing staff and physicians realize that families and patients also need rest in order to recover, function normally, and maintain their sanity. Recently, the American Medical Association mandated that the number of hours that trainee physicians worked per week needed to be reduced in order for them to make better decisions and function more efficiently. So it should come as no surprise that families become obnoxious and lash out at nursing staff and others when they are overly tired and sleep deprived.

The solution is care designed around the patient and family, not the convenience of doctors and nurses—family-centered care. We introduced some of the following initial suggestions to the care plan of the Heart Institute at Le Bonheur Children's Hospital in Memphis in 2010:

1. Make everyone aware of the problem. "Everyone" includes the physicians, nursing staff and nurse aids, respiratory therapists, cleaning staff, and so on.
2. Schedule routine blood draws and x-rays for 7:00 a.m., not 4:00 a.m. when the patient and family are finally getting some sleep.
3. Schedule breathing treatments and medications for the night to be given at 9:00 p.m., not 1:00 a.m., whenever possible.
4. Empower nursing staff to skip the 2:00 a.m. vital signs if the remote monitoring systems, such as continuous pulse, oxygen levels, oximeter, and heart rhythm, are within normal limits.
5. If a patient is asleep, do not wake him or her unless it is vitally important.
6. If labs are needed, make sure that *all* the labs are drawn at the same time *once a day* so that the patient is not poked more often.

7. Open and close doors to the room manually; do not pull the door open and allow it to close with a bang.
8. Speak in a soft voice or a whisper, even when you are outside the room or in the corridor.

Some of these suggestions seem obvious to everyone. They certainly seemed obvious to me in 2010. But they will change the accent of the care we provide from "patient care" to "patient caring." And they will be appreciated by the endless families who have to go through this every week.

"Embrace your pain—it's the only thing that separates the living from the dead. I never saw a dead patient complain of pain."

Although I absolutely do not tolerate my patients experiencing pain after surgery, especially infants and children, I would round on my older adult patients, who invariably complained of all kinds of aches and pains when they were getting ready to be discharged, and each time they mentioned a new pain, I would respond, "Good." Then I would add what is obvious to many of us who are caregivers, "Only dead people have *no* pain."

41

Demonstrating Cardiac Surgery Can Be Disastrous

One of my favorite cardiac surgery stories was shared with me by my good friend Professor Giovanni Stellin, the chief of cardiac surgery at the University of Padua—ostensibly the oldest medical school in the world and the one where Galileo taught centuries ago.

An incident occurred in the mid-1980s, when the then chief of cardiac surgery was doing a coronary artery bypass operation. The surgery was not going well. He was trying to sew the left internal mammary artery (LIMA) to an obstructed coronary artery. Although this operation was commonly done in the United States, it was apparently still a relatively new technique in Europe. There was an audience of visiting cardiac surgeons in the operating room with him, all watching him demonstrate how to do this delicate operation. As I alluded to earlier, using the LIMA to bypass the obstructed coronary arteries is currently the standard operation throughout the world, but at that time it was known as "that stupid operation, which only the Americans can do." So many surgeons were watching this famous, well-known surgeon and European professor demonstrating how to do it, but the surgery was a bit of a mess. The LIMA was very friable, and each time a suture was placed through it to anchor it to the diseased coronary artery of the patient, it somehow tore out and another suture was needed to fix the previous suture, and so on and so on it went. The professor was drenched in perspiration and a little agitated, but finally he got the LIMA sewn to the coronary artery successfully.

He straightened up, stretched his aching back, and looked up to the ceiling as if thanking God, and he whispered something under his breath. Immediately, his assistant surgeon took the high-pressure wall suction apparatus and placed it against the difficult, just-completed anastomosis of the LIMA-to-coronary artery. In a split second, the strong suction ripped the delicate LIMA off of the anastomosis, totally disrupting it. In fact, not only had it sucked the LIMA off of the coronary anastomosis, it had severed the LIMA and sucked the entire pedicle artery off the chest wall and into the suction reservoir, which was hanging on the side of the wall of the operating room. This was where discarded blood and fluid from the surgery were also collected.

In total disbelief, the furious professor, struggling to control himself in front of his guests, yelled at his assistant, "Why did you do that?" The distraught assistant replied, "I thought you said, 'Suck it,' sir." The professor screamed back at him, "I said, 'Fuck it,' not 'Suck it'!"

No coming back from that one! Not even Galileo could come back after that one. No one in the operating room dared to murmur or laugh then, but hundreds of cardiac surgeons around the world have subsequently roared with laughter in pubs around the world. And yes, the assistant cardiac surgeon shall remain nameless.

42

"Tiredness Is a State of Mind— and Sleep Is Overrated"

Surgeons often work very long hours, and successful pediatric cardiac surgeons most often work extremely long hours. Some surgeries may last ten to fourteen hours and require an additional four to six hours to settle down a patient in the intensive care unit. I once spent five days and four nights without leaving the bedside of a baby in Harley Street Clinic while working for Professor Marc DeLeval in London.

The unwritten rule is that the junior surgeons or trainees do not leave for home before the senior surgeon leaves. Consequently, on many occasions, I would look into the bleary, bloodshot eyes of a resident or fellow and utter the immortalized lines with a wink: "Tiredness is a state of mind, and sleep is overrated." As I get older, this statement becomes less and less accurate.

43

Parents' Night Out

Some parents are more stressed out than most others after their babies have cardiac surgery. It's not a racial thing, a social thing, or a religious thing—at least not completely. It seems rather to be related to the nuclear family dynamics, the support or lack of support, or in many cases, the excessive expectations and pressure on new parents by the rest of the family. Always, there is just the sheer exhaustion of feeding your baby after major surgery, burping him and putting him down, and having him woken up by nursing staff to check his vital signs, give him medicine, or draw labs from his veins. After three or four days, parents reach a breaking point.

It was a situation like this that was evolving with a young family from Jackson, Tennessee, in early February 2009. Each minor incident became bigger and bigger in the perception of the parents, and tempers started to become frayed. It was a Friday afternoon when I recognized the warning signs, and suddenly I had an idea. My family was still in Birmingham, Alabama, and I would not see them that weekend. I was on call, anyway.

So I told the parents that between six and nine o'clock that evening I would babysit their baby for them in the hospital, and that would allow them to both be away from the hospital at the same time. They needed to go have a romantic supper together, get a room somewhere, have a date, and for a brief period in time, forget about their baby. I would take care of him personally. (When babies are in a regular room, not in the ICU, at least one parent needs to be with the baby at all times.)

They looked at me as though I was crazy. Then the mother wept uncontrollably. She dressed up as best she could, she put on makeup and lipstick (I think the nursing staff lent her some of theirs), and her husband picked her up and took her out. I carried her baby around with me everywhere I went, just as I promised I would. For a moment, I wondered what would happen if the security staff stopped me. Here was a man who spoke with an accent, who was not dressed as a doctor is expected to dress, and who was carrying around a baby hospital patient with a name tag different from that of the man on a Friday night without a nurse or parent accompanying him.

Nevertheless, the parents returned at nine thirty refreshed, smiling, and happy, and they didn't have that harried, cabin fever, "I can't cope any more" look about them. They were so grateful! And that is how Parents' Night Out started at Le Bonheur Children's Hospital. Initially, nurses volunteered to do the babysitting for needy families on their off time. Subsequently, the parents volunteer association took up this mission, and a year later, parents with babies in the hospital regularly get a Friday night out on the town courtesy of the other parents who have benefitted from this program and numerous other parents who understand the need and empathize with the cause.

As with so many major breakthroughs in medicine, it all started by chance as a way of helping others through a particularly difficult time, the way our Savior helps us through our difficult times, regularly.

44

The Comfort Cloth and Cardiac Surgery

Everyone needs a comfort cloth, even babies—especially babies going through heart surgery. Adults have a favorite couch they lie on when they get home after work, a special soap opera on TV they watch with a cup of coffee or a glass of wine, special food they nibble on, or a special piece of music they listen to—the Chopin nocturnes, Bach's Cello Suites, or Beethoven's sonatas. Or they may buy or pick a special flower. Let's just analyze this for a moment: the couch satisfies the sense of touch; the soap opera satisfies the sense of sight; the chocolate satisfies the sense of taste; the music satisfies the sense of hearing; and the flower satisfies the sense of smell. These are the five senses common to all living beings.

Which sense is most important to *you*? I don't know. But wouldn't it be wonderful if we could anticipate it and fulfill it, especially when you are feeling miserable? Or better still, what if we could accommodate many of them, or all of them, when you feel particularly down or feel you need to be pampered? On Valentine's Day, for example, you get roses, chocolates, and teddy bear and then go out for dinner and the opera—all five senses satisfied!

So why would your baby, infant, or child be any different from you, especially when he or she comes out of major cardiac surgery? I could never understand why fellow colleagues, health care providers, hospitals, and nursing staff could not understand this or my overwhelming desire to provide comfort for my patients with as much enthusiasm as I have for the delicate surgeries I do. The University of Alabama at Birmingham (UAB), formerly the mecca of cardiac surgery, just couldn't get it, which was a major source of disagreement between us that ultimately resulted in my resignation. Dr. Cindy Barret, a young cardiac intensivist hired from Harvard to help with the postoperative care of my patients, was vehemently opposed to these views.

That was the predominant motivation for my move to Le Bonheur Children's Hospital in Memphis, Tennessee. When I interviewed with the president and CEO, Meri Armour, she got it immediately. Having a background as a neonatal nurse, she not only got it; she imposed it and made sure that everyone either bought into this radical change in quality of care provided or understood that they would need to find different employment. With that level of commitment, everything started to fall into place, and my dream of a better, safer, more wholesome, proactive level of care came to fruition.

So, this is the product of that commitment: this is the comfort cloth for babies who have heart surgery at Le Bonheur and hopefully throughout the world sometime soon.

When the babies come out of the operating room, soft eye pads are put on their eyes to keep out the harsh lights and the heat from the overhead heating lamps (imagine lying in a tanning booth without eye covers). When they start to awaken, the lights in the room are turned down to a twilight level, not bright. Special padded earphones are placed on their ears to keep out the noxious noises of the ICU, with the alarms going off and the beeping of the monitors and the strange voices. Mozart or the parents' voices singing, reading, or talking to the babies is piped through the earphones. The hands of the nurses and physicians are warmed up before they touch the baby to avoid startling him or her, and a favorite blankie or pillowcase that the mother has slept on is placed against the baby's face so that he or she can smell the mommy. If the infant or child is older, the mother is encouraged to climb onto the bed with her baby so that she can cuddle him or her, even as early as six hours after a complex surgery. (See pictures.)

Parents stay in or even sleep in the room in the ICU and on the floor ward room twenty-four hours a day and participate in physician rounds daily. Patients are not transferred out of the ICU until the parents are comfortable with being discharged. Needless to say, "When Mama is happy, everyone is happy." When patients have their comfort cloths, they heal quicker and with fewer complications, and hopefully, with less long-term sequelae related to emotional trauma, fear, and pain. As a result, we as surgeons and intensivists have provided more than just plumbing and documentation to our patients. We have cared fully for them.

45

The Mexican Policeman

Police officers in the United States can be rather intimidating to foreigners; in fact, they usually are! In the aftermath of 9/11, with the ensuing heightened state of airport security worldwide, they were especially so.

When we disembarked from the Continental Airlines 737 in Los Cabos, Mexico, the afternoon before Christmas 2001, the excited planeload of sun-seeking tourists became suddenly quiet at the foot of the ramp. On the airport tarmac was a foreboding Mexican *polizei* (policeman). He stood with his arms folded across his chest, the smoke curling up from a cheap cigarette in his hand. His desert-tan uniform appeared well worn, a peaked military cap was tucked low over his forehead, and a silver badge shone in the sun. His face wore a practiced expressionless look, his sunken and sallow cheeks beaded with sweat, and his eyes were covered with wraparound sky-blue shades. Clint Eastwood in *Dirty Harry* came to mind, as he dared anyone to give him half a reason to use the pistol hanging at his side.

I swallowed and looked around for my wife and teenage kids. This was not a good time for spur-of-the-moment jokes or trying out our rudimentary Spanish. We shuffled somberly past this security policeman to the immigration lounge, single file, feeling uneasy and guilty of something, though we weren't sure what.

What struck me most as I passed this intimidating representative—ostensibly of safety and security—in a foreign country was a small lapel pin on his jacket, hidden among the other attestations to his bravery, ruthlessness, or whatever. This one I immediately recognized. It was red, white, and blue and said, "Proud to be American." I struggled to suppress a smile and a chuckle until I was safely out of sight. I wondered if he could read English or just thought it looked important.

46

The Vulnerability of Vanity

We are so dependent on others' opinions of ourselves for our well-being. This is probably good in many ways, though, especially when we are trying to establish ourselves in our careers or when we feel important. Most women like to buy a new dress before a grand ball, and most men will wear a new shirt or suit if they should have the honor of, say, meeting the governor or some dignitary. However, sometimes this aspect of human nature can be our downfall too, as illustrated in this true story.

Dave Richens was a young British cardiac surgeon whom we had invited to Cape Town to give a lecture on coronary angioscopy, something he had started doing in the United Kingdom to evaluate the quality of coronary bypass anastomoses. It was one of the first of such invitations he had received, perhaps even the very first time he had been invited to speak in a foreign country, and at the center where Christiaan Barnard had performed the world's first heart transplant. This was a big honor for a senior registrar from England, and it was important to make a good first impression.

So toward the end of the thirteen-hour flight to Cape Town, when the plane started its descent, Dave went to the aircraft's bathroom to freshen up. Well, Dave was about six feet three, a big fella, and planned to change into some fresh clothes. He stripped down to his underwear in the confines of the rather cramped airplane bathroom. Since he was a little nervous, it was summertime, and the flight had been very full and long, he decided to spray some deodorant all over his body. Well, this was just after the airlines had banned smoking on all flights, which the population generally felt was an infringement on their personal freedom (to smoke); therefore, many people resorted to ducking into the toilet stalls to have a quick cigarette. The flight attendants were alerted to this and were very strict about enforcing the no-smoking policy, and the bathrooms were fitted with smoke detectors. However, the early smoke detectors frequently confused the fumes from deodorants and antiperspirants with the smoke from cigarettes. So there Dave was in his underpants, all six feet three of him, when the smoke detector went off, and the flight attendants—with the vociferous encouragement of the multitude of passengers all dying to have a cigarette—swarmed to the toilet stall demanding that he open the door immediately. The more Dave tried to persuade them through the closed door that he was innocent, while also trying desperately to put his legs back in his trousers, the more they pushed the door inward. Since Dave was standing with his back to the door and was bending over trying to put his feet into his trouser legs, each time they pushed the door, his head all but ended up in the toilet bowl. He lost the battle. They forced the door open and pulled him out into the aisle in his now decidedly less-than-fresh underwear while they checked the toilet. All the passengers were craning their necks to get a glimpse of the person at the center of the commotion. Dave says that in his embarrassment he couldn't decide whether to first cover his ding-dong or his face.

No sooner had he gotten dressed than the plane touched down in Cape Town, and I was there to meet him. He looked somewhat disheveled and smelled somewhat rancid, even for someone who had just completed a long flight, and even for a cardiac surgeon. But what I remember most clearly is that the first thing he said to me when we shook hands was, "Where can I get a scotch?" I wondered whether he meant a shot or the whole bottle.